MORE PRAISE FOR *NOTHING LEFT OVER:*

"I can think of no greater praise than to say this is an honest book; it helps us understand what the values of 'simple living' are really menat to impart in a complicated and unsimple world, not just theoretically, but in the details of our everyday existence."

—JACOB NEEDLEMAN, AUTHOR OF *THE AMERICAN SOUL*

"I find myself thrown into a state of wonder that a life story so authentic in its telling and so fascinating to read could be lived amid the turmoil of a modern metropolis."

—THOMAS BERRY, AUTHOR OF *THE GREAT WORK*

"Read Nothing Left Over *slowly in a quiet place. Let it lead you to do some interior housekeeping. Live with those changes for a while, and then return to the book for another gentle suggestion, and then another, about what it really means to be contained and satisfied.*"

—*SPIRITUALITY & HEALTH*

"This is the elegance of the book: the idea that any moment contains all that we really need to know in order to live simply and plainly; every instance presents an opportunity to refine our awareness so that we can be present and of service to others."

—*TURNING WHEEL*

"Nothing Left Over *reveals an independently won spiritual maturity. Readers will appreciate her practical advice on attitudes toward everyday life.*"

—*SHAMBHALA SUN*

Nothing Left Over

A PLAIN AND SIMPLE LIFE

Toinette Lippe

JEREMY P. TARCHER • PENGUIN

a member of Penguin Group (USA) Inc.

New York

Grateful acknowledgment is made to Alfred A. Knopf, a division of Random House, Inc., for permission to use chapter I I from *Tao Te Ching*, by Lao Tsu, translated by Gia-fu Feng and Jane English. Copyright © 1972 by Gia-fu Feng and Jane English.

Most Tarcher/Penguin books are available at special quantity discounts for bulk purchases for sales promotions, premiums, fund-raising, and educational needs. Special books or book excerpts also can be created to fit specific needs. For details, write Penguin Group (USA) Inc. Special Markets, 375 Hudson Street, New York, NY 10014.

Jeremy P. Tarcher/Penguin
a member of
Penguin Group (USA) Inc.
375 Hudson Street
New York, NY 10014
www.penguin.com

Library of Congress Cataloging-in-Publication Data

Lippe, Toinette, date.
Nothing left over : a plain and simple life / Toinette Lippe.
p. cm.
ISBN 1-58542-160-X
I. Simplicity. 2. Conduct of life. 3. Lippe, Toinette, date. I. Title.
BJ1496 .L57   2002   2001052582
179'.9—dc21

ISBN 1-58542-305-X (paperback edition)
Printed in the United States of America
1   3   5   7   9   10   8   6   4   2

Book design by Marysarah Quinn

For Joel Fotinos, my publisher,

who caught me on the cusp,

inviting me to reflect on the lessons I have learned so far

and watch what happens as I enter the unknown future.

Without this gift I would still be living an unexamined life.

Now I find myself perched on the fulcrum of the present.

I offer him my love and thanks.

With deep gratitude I acknowledge my debt to numberless friends, acquaintances, and even enemies—without whose teaching I would not have been able to write this book.

Contents

Experience is the fuel;

I would live my life burning it up as I go along,

so that at the end nothing is left unused,

so that every piece of it has been consumed in the work.

MAY SARTON, *Plant Dreaming Deep*

Nothing Left Over

ONE

Teach Me What Life Is For

It wasn't until I was seventeen that I began to wonder what life was for. I had gone to boarding school at four for a year (because my English parents felt I would be safer there than staying with them on an RAF base during World War II), and after that I was cared for at home by a strict Victorian nanny, the daughter of a Royal Marine, who had been hired to look after my little brother. When I was ten, I went away to boarding school once more, and for seven years I worked hard and tried to do whatever was expected of me. Eventually, I passed all my exams with flying colors; but instead of being accepted at a university where I had dreamed of exploring the universe and finding the friends I had never had at high school, I found myself with a state scholarship but no place at any college. It was hard in those days for a girl to gain admission. I believe I could have got in if I had said that I wanted to teach. But I thought that the whole point of going to college was to discover what you might want to do from the vast array of possibilities. Why would you make up your mind before you even knew what these might be? I felt that I couldn't make such a commitment at the outset, and so when I was asked whether I wanted to be a teacher, I answered, "I don't know."

Since I wasn't going to a university like everyone else, there I was with the whole of my life before me, and I didn't know what direction to take. I remember asking my parents what life was all about. What was everyone supposed to be doing? How could I decide how to spend my life if no one had ever explained the point of it? My education had filled my head with information that might or might not turn out to be useful, but there had never been any discussion of why we were learning all this. Now I was launched, so to speak, yet without any guiding principles.

My parents were alarmed at my questions. They never seemed to have had any doubt about what their function was. They met while working with the poor in the East End of London and went on to become mayor of Harrow (each of them in turn). Their lives were devoted to public service. I didn't see this as necessarily the only path, although I respected their approach. When I started demanding answers, they summoned the family doctor, the genial Dr. Waller (house calls were still possible in those days), to whom I tearfully posed my questions. He listened for a few minutes and then told me that people just didn't ask questions like those. They weren't appropriate. He reported to my father and mother that I was suffering from a nervous breakdown and prescribed a program of rest and exercise (I was not naturally athletic but soon found myself enrolled in fencing, skating, swimming, and "keep-fit" classes). I had been about to set off for Switzerland to become the secretary to the director of the Swiss Everest Foundation, but Dr. Waller decided that I had worked too hard at my exams and should not be even more stressed by earning my living in another language in a foreign country. So my questions were squelched, and I was made to feel as though I had done something unforgivable by even raising them.

I bring all this up because I suspect it may be a far from uncommon experience, even if the details of the dilemma are different for each of us. Our parents and teachers try to do their best for us, but either there never seems to be a suitable moment to address questions like these or they themselves have not found the answers and so hesitate to offer advice for fear of being more of a hindrance than a help. It is a little like the way sex education was then: no one spoke about it, and it was assumed that each person would discover the facts for him- or herself. There is, of course, one other possibility, and that is that a great many people simply never allow themselves to voice these questions. The aim of modern education seems to be to equip us to be suitably employed so that we can support ourselves and our families. And once we are employed, the idea is to get through our working lives so that we can enjoy ourselves in our retirement. How on earth did society lose sight of its reason for existence? And how can we know what to do now, in this moment, if we don't know where we are going?

After three months of exercise and no intellectual stimulation, my questions faded into the background, and I set about earning my living like everyone else. Then, quite by chance it seemed, I started attending evening classes at the School of Economic Science (not to be confused with the London School of Economics). It came about this way: I was dating a rather diffident young legal student who mentioned that he planned to sign up for philosophy classes and asked me if I would like to accompany him. In the London Underground there were these plain black-and-white posters with the word *Philosophy* printed in large navy blue letters. (In those days I was unaware that this word meant "love of wisdom.") While I waited for the train, I would study the few paragraphs of course description and was always puzzled by the fact that afterward I couldn't articulate what I had read. Even now I cannot tell you what was on the poster, but I was so intrigued by this phenomenon that I decided to enroll together with Anthony and find out what the course had to offer.

I have to say that I found the first two lectures rather boring and simplistic. The course was taught through the Socratic method: raising questions. Answers were not often forthcoming, but at last many of the questions that had been troubling me were being asked. We had a rather benevolent middle-aged tutor who listened carefully to the response of each student and then smiled and said, "Yes." I noticed that he had responded this way to two diametrically opposite answers, and so I challenged him. "When I say 'Yes,'" he replied, "I mean that I've heard you, not that I agree with what you say."

Halfway through the first term, we were invited to sign up for the following one. At the coffee break, small groups of students were discussing their plans, and I hovered at the edge of one of these. There was one man in our class I particularly respected. He was tall, good-looking, intelligent, and solid as a rock. He appeared to know his own mind, and I always appreciated what he had to say. He remarked that although he himself had not yet found much of value in the classes, he had a close friend, an older man, who had been attending them for years. If his friend had found something worthwhile here and he had not, perhaps the fault was his. He said that he was going to sign up for the next term to see if he could discover what his old friend had found. And I signed up also, just because this logic was so persuasive. At least I had found a community where it was acceptable to ask important questions.

I remained in this organization for a considerable number of years, studying the philosophy of many of the world's great traditions, and what I heard and put into practice there laid the groundwork for the rest of my life. At that time I believed that "the truth" was available only through this one conduit. Now I see that it is available anywhere and everywhere. But I probably would not have realized this without my early schooling in this particular discipline.

It was my friend and publisher, Joel Fotinos, who dreamed up the idea for this book. The thought would never have occurred to me on my own. We were having dinner one night, I was telling him of my plans to leave full-time employment, and he instantly suggested that I write a book for him with this title. Once I had got over the shock, the notion seemed irresistible. When I stopped to consider it, I realized that everything I do is governed by the principle of not having anything left over. Still, I'm baffled that he was able to size me up so accurately.

I see now that living economically and wanting to be of service to other people and share with them whatever has come my way have always been themes for me. When I first came to the United States, I met with the head of the fledgling New York philosophy school, which went under a different name than the School of Economic Science, and she asked me, "What do you want from us?" I was taken aback by this question because both at home and in the school's parent organization in London, I could not recall anyone ever asking me what I wanted. As far back as I remembered, I was simply told what to do, and usually I did it. I don't wish to imply that I was a yes-person. I certainly challenged authority a great deal, but this took a certain amount of courage because challenge was not considered an option by Those-in-Charge. (This was England fifty years ago. In the United States there are always so many options . . .)

For a moment there was silence as I tried to collect my thoughts, and then I said, "I just want to be useful." I understand now that this desire has characterized my whole life. I like things to be put to good use. For me, economy is all. I never buy or cook any more than is necessary. I am always going through my closets to see what I can pass on to someone else. I feel guilty if I am not using whatever I own—books, sweaters, shoes, you name it. And when I went through my files to see if I had ever written anything on the subject of economy, I found a quote from May Sarton (the epigraph of this book) that I had squirreled away five years before. Come to think of it, none of this should have surprised me, since I began my training at a place called the School of Economic Science! (The school had begun by teaching the economics of the American Henry George, author of *Progress and Poverty*, and had gone on to add philosophy to its curriculum. I never found the economic aspect of what was taught there very appealing—or so I thought until now. I'd always been under the impression that I had gone there for the philosophy.)

As I thought about it, I realized that the result of gathering about you only what you need and relinquishing everything else is self-sufficiency—a lack of emotional neediness. This is another way of saying that it is wise to be satisfied with what you have. Lately,

I have been mulling over the word *content*. I find it wonderful that it means both "that which is contained" and also "being satisfied." Both meanings come from the past participle of the Latin verb *continere*. Contentment is a peaceful and unruffled state, but nowadays it is all too rare.

So everything you read in these pages is an exploration of how to live so that supply does not exceed demand or consumption; how to share whatever you may have with everyone else, not holding anything back in a miserly way; and how to trust that the universe will respond to you in the same way that you respond to it.

I visited the island of Bali in 1986, and my most enduring impression of it is its fecundity. Bali is located seven degrees from the equator, but since it is a small island, it never seems to get too hot. It does, however, rain every day for a little while. The result is that there doesn't seem to be a square inch of land where things aren't growing in profusion. And, in many ways, that is how it is with the world. Everything is available in profusion. It is just not always obvious when you are not in Bali.

I had always thought that I lived a plain and simple life until I began to write about it, and then I became amazed and almost overcome by the wealth and quality of my experiences. I now feel very blessed.

I have tried to put down my observations on how the world works so that you, too, can share in this abundance. In order to get back to the essentials, we must first identify what they are. Only then are we in a position to do something about them. What follows is not so much about what needs to take place at the physical level—practical instructions on what to do or not to do—as about what goes on in the mind. Don't try to change things on the outside—in the "real" world. The work has to be done on the inside. It is a kind of interior housekeeping. Each time you drop an old attitude or habit, it is like spring cleaning: more space becomes available. There is room to move about and examine the situation from a new perspective, and everything feels freer and lighter. If you clarify the mind and relinquish some of the curious ideas that have become lodged there (most of the time we aren't even aware of them), then you will be free to enjoy all the glorious things that are in the physical realm. So here are a few principles for clearing the mind of clutter.

TWO

Taking Stock

It is August and just over a week since I quit corporate America and launched out on my own. For the last eleven years I have juggled two almost full-time jobs at Random House with only half an assistant—selling reprint rights for Alfred A. Knopf (something that became so familiar to me after thirty-two years that I felt as though I could do it in my sleep) and publishing nine books a year at Bell Tower, a spiritual imprint I set up as part of Harmony Books in 1989. Earlier this year I admitted to myself that I was unenjoying a great deal of each day, and I decided to stop living my work and start living my life. I have taken my pension and made an arrangement to continue editing my Bell Tower books as an independent contractor.

I planned to set things up in a corner of my living room so that my home office would be almost as invisible as my small, elderly television set. Perhaps that will eventually happen but, for the time being, it is just not possible. The office is there, but it is certainly not invisible. My son, Adam, graduated from college in May and announced that he didn't want to live at home. I supported his decision (after having had the place more or less to myself for the last four years, I have grown to like living alone) but pointed out that first he needed a job and a checking account. I suggested he wait to get an apartment until he had settled into a job.

Unfortunately, he was miserable in his first job (not surprising since he was trying to sell telephone service door-to-door), quit after just a few weeks, and is now a little at sea as to what to do next. So it looks as though it will be some months before he and all his accumulated possessions from college will leave the apartment. Currently, every closet is jammed with his goods and chattels. And then I purchased a computer, printer, and scanner for my new life and acquired with them three

huge boxes I dare not abandon for a year in case anything goes wrong. After which I brought back from
the office nine boxes of my own stuff that I felt I
needed to set up shop. So every available surface—
windowsills, tables, and floor space—is stacked with
files and books and manuscripts. This is hard for
someone like me who thrives on a great deal of empty
space. But this *is* the situation, and there is no choice
but to relax into it and not fret.

This new phase of my life has forced me to reexam-
ine and question the smallest details: Why do I do this
rather than that? Is there a real reason for it? Or is it
just the encrustation of habit? This happened once
before in 1964 when I came to live in the United
States. I had thought I was coming here to discover
what America was like. Instead, it was myself I discovered. For a short while, silhouetted against the back-
drop of a new country and culture, I was able to see
who I thought I was more clearly than ever before.

Human beings are creatures of habit. What normally happens is that we develop bad habits, but it is
not so hard to develop good habits instead. Once these
are set in motion, they operate on their own. In some
ways this is a blessing because the moving mind (the

part of the brain that learns how to perform physical movements) takes over physical and mental activities, and we come to rely on it. This is what I hope will take place with all this new equipment with which I have encumbered myself. There is a jungle of wires and tefillin-like black plugs seething beneath my desk— evidence of a terrifying amount of electricity being consumed in the name of simplicity. At the moment I am still in the learning stage, trying to figure out exactly what is in the computer Dell shipped me and how to make good use of it. Presumably, at some point this will all recede into my moving memory and become second nature. However, after sixty-one years of living, far too many things have become automatic for me. Half the time I do not even realize that I am doing them, and I welcome the opportunity to take a fresh look at everything.

We get very attached to our habits, and it can be amusing to try to dislodge some of them occasionally. As we grow older, we tend to close down our options. We think of it as refining our taste. We prefer broccoli to cabbage and cauliflower, so we gradually stop buying cabbage and cauliflower. There is nothing wrong with eating broccoli (my favorite vegetable), but a variety is always healthier. It is not a very good idea to eat broccoli every night of your life.

We place our slippers in a particular way under a chair. We can no longer even imagine placing them any other way. It is okay to eliminate unnecessary things, but we need to keep an eye open to make sure that we don't go overboard. I noticed that I always hold the telephone in my right hand. The other day I decided to pick it up with my left hand. It felt very strange. The telephone was heavy in my hand. I pressed it too hard against my ear. I didn't seem able to relax with it the way I normally do. Also, I wasn't used to listening with the other ear, and there seemed to be a great deal of echo either in the receiver or in my head. When I thought about this for a moment, I realized that all my life I have been overtaxing one ear and causing pressure on it. Also, I have not been using 50 percent of my listening (and holding) capacity. This really woke me up. We need to be flexible—willing to cross our legs the opposite way for a change, open the refrigerator door with the other hand. We have to guard against not becoming rigid. Flexibility offers a slender tree the freedom to sway in the wind, and so it is with us.

Since I am someone who has lived a very orderly life up to now, I had nursed the idea that in the future I would not be so rigid. My days would proceed naturally, and I would not set aside special times for this and that. I would cope with e-mail (something I had not permitted in the house before), the phone and fax, work on manuscripts as the occasion demanded, and an opportunity would spontaneously arise each day for me to write a portion of this book. I would never feel pressured again. There would be time for walks and expeditions, meals with friends, joining a community garden in Riverside Park that I had long admired, tai chi chuan, a second period of meditation in the late afternoon, and so on.

I had been invited to write this book at the beginning of April, and now it was August. It had taken all these months to organize things so that I would have the time to write the book. I had to give up my job at Knopf before I could take on another project. So I thought that on the first day of my newfound freedom, there would come a moment when I would just start writing the first chapter.

But this did not happen. Each day I was busy from

seven in the morning until Adam returned at the end of the day. It rained a great deal, so I did not go out much. There was always more Bell Tower work to do; it was right there in front of me, and there never seemed to be a natural break when I could turn to what I saw as my own work. After four days of this, I realized that I had trained myself for forty-three years to put my employer's interests before my own, and this was going to be a tough habit to break. The first lesson in my new life was perhaps how to establish boundaries.

I thought back to the days when I had begun to meditate and remembered how at first it was so difficult to fit two half-hours into an already crowded day. Then it became clear that if you waited for a space to appear in your schedule, it never did. But if you meditated before the day began and again at the beginning of the evening, there was never any problem fitting everything else in. So I determined that in the weeks ahead I simply had to sit down at the computer early in the day and not peek at my e-mail until the time for writing was over—not that I needed to set a specific time to start and finish but that I had to take care of this one thing, my writing, before all the demands of the day claimed my attention.

· · ·

That was August, and I was full of good intentions. Now it is February. It has been just over six months since I abandoned a full-time job for the freedom of a life of my own, and it is *hard*. For all these months I have been coasting along on the energy accumulated over a lifetime of push, push, push. I had had a full (too full), active, and successful professional life, and now that I have broken loose from the old mold, I am in limbo. I am no longer being driven by outside circumstances, and inertia has set in to some extent. This is truly a bleak, dry, and uneasy time. In my previous life I was, of course, usually on automatic, reacting to outside stimuli.

Whoever I talk to or whatever I read points out that the way to get going again is to make myself a schedule and stick to it. As the months trickled by I noticed that, although I planned to start writing at 8 A.M. and round off the day by practicing tai chi chuan at 5 P.M., neither of these things ever happened. Yes, it is possible to schedule every moment of the day and not allow yourself any wiggle room. That way I would certainly get things done, but would I be any more present while I was doing them than I had been in my old job? I do not want to exchange one kind of servitude for another. Not that you can't choose to be present at any moment, but being present does tend not to happen if you get pulled or pushed into the next activity through sheer force of habit. I know only too well that I can have a bath, get dressed, do my mini-stint of yoga, eat breakfast, and listen to the news on National Public Radio, without really knowing what I am doing.

Early on in my time at the philosophy school, we were instructed to pause between actions and remember who we were. One of the reasons for this was to prevent the energy from one task from being carried forward into the next. If you make a clean break when you finish something and come to a full stop, then you can start fresh with whatever is necessary for the next action. This made an inordinate amount of sense to me, and I resolved to introduce the practice into my life. That was over thirty years ago, and I haven't managed it yet because I have always been moving so fast that I have been unable to come to a stop. This is a terrible admission for someone who believes she has a lot of willpower, but it is true. I have failed absolutely, so it is not surprising that I am having such a difficult time with the two things I have recently tried to add to my schedule.

It occurs to me that in my old life I was like one of those little Volkswagens, beetling along the highway en route to events other people had organized. In this new life I am determined to leave the day open and experiment with formlessness. I know this is harder than making myself a new timetable, but I have a long history of doing things the hard way, if only to prove that it is possible. I believe that operating without a regular schedule is the only way I will discover the space around and between things and events. In the past I led a tethered life, and now perhaps I can learn to glide on the available air currents.

So: I no longer feel as though I am running my life. I am not running after it or ahead of it. It is just running on its own, and if I stay in the present from time to time, I catch a glimpse of what is approaching and am ready to welcome it when it arrives. You could say that I am here expecting the unexpected.

To the extent to which I am able I am trying to live without props. This doesn't mean that I don't plan anything (this is, after all, New York in the twenty-first century). At my age I suspect that it isn't possible to change the time I awake naturally in the morning (5:30 to 5:45 A.M.), or the time my eyelids close in the evening (10-ish). Anyway, I don't think that I need to alter those things. There is plenty of time during the day between waking and sleeping, and if I can relax my grip on all those hours, perhaps I will also find a way to make a shift between the sheets.

What it means is that I am not dragooning myself to do things. This way, I don't have to deal with the regret that will definitely arise when I don't manage to do them. For instance, I have just started a Japanese brush-painting class, which is something I have been meaning to do for longer than I care to admit. On my shelf I have a slew of books on the subject. Over the years different friends have given me not only books but also rice paper, brushes, an inkstone, and sticks of red and black ink. I never asked for any of this stuff, but my friends were convinced that I would enjoy brush painting. I even have a manuscript a would-be author sent me from California in 1985, complete with brush-writing equipment (this was for Chinese brush writing and painting). The manuscript arrived unsolicited with a letter that encouraged me to follow the instructions in the teaching manual. "There is no

SASE," it continued. "If you like the experience, think about publishing the book. If the answer is still no, just let me know." The author and I wrote back and forth for some time and eventually he said, "I am moving you from my book publisher file to my correspondence course file." I never actually started grinding the ink and using the brushes, however, and neither did I publish his book.

Then, last fall, I went to China in a group led by Kazuaki Tanahashi, a master Japanese brush painter now living in California. We were following in the footsteps of Dogen, the thirteenth-century founder of Soto Zen Buddhism, but Kaz initiated us into painting the *enso*, or circle, for several mornings in Shaoxing (the Orchid Pavilion there is renowned for its calligraphers, particularly Wang Xizhi, the inventor of Chinese running script, which is like clouds floating in the sky), Hangzhou, and elsewhere. Kaz showed us how to grind the ink (hold the ink stick vertically and make sure its whole surface is in contact with the inkstone as you dilute the ink with water) and then draw a circle on the flimsy paper. He demonstrated how to do it but didn't give us any verbal instructions. Later I questioned one of my fellow travelers who had once taken a course with him, and he said that Kaz had told him that the brush should be vertical and the mouth horizontal. (I think I have that right. This meant that the mouth should be in a half smile, which certainly helps to keep you relaxed.)

While we were in Hangzhou we paid a visit to the Shi-lin Seal Engravers Society on an island in the graceful West Lake, where many of the group had individual chops made (these are the traditional seals with which painters and calligraphers sign their work). I couldn't imagine that my work would ever be good enough to sign, so while I waited for the others, I made a momentous purchase of my own: a set of three beautiful brushes in a green brocade box.

On my return to New York early in November, I put them on the shelf with my growing collection and eyed them ruefully from time to time. Then, in January, I was in SoHo at lunchtime, and I walked past a little storefront with a sign that said KOHO SCHOOL OF SUMI-E. Outside was a bunch of flyers, so I took one home and read it from end to end. It sounded very forbidding, but it did offer the possibility of watching a class before signing up for a ten-week course. A few weeks later I was again in the vicinity and the lights were on in the store, so I walked in. The gracious Japanese-American teacher and her cat who greeted me were both very welcoming, and so I decided to come a few days later to observe the Sunday-morning class. While waiting for the other students to arrive, I learned that Koho was almost eighty years old and had established her school on the corner of Houston and Macdougal Streets twenty years before—around the time I had started gathering brushes, ink, and books. I think that this fact brought home to me that I couldn't afford to wait any longer. I had already lost the possibility of learning from her for the last twenty years. Who knew how much longer she would be teaching? I made a commitment to join the class the following weekend and now, after three lessons, am happily experimenting with bamboo leaves and stalks. Plum blossom and pine trees to follow.

It is fascinating that I have chosen to study this particular discipline without really knowing why. Just yesterday, I came across this quote by Motoi Oi: "The aim of the Sumi-e artist is not the reproduction of the subject matter but the elimination of the inessential." The book in which I found the quote, *The Book of Bamboo,* by David Farrelly, goes on to say that the aim is "not to record every rock on the mountain or each leaf in the grove, but to capture—with a spare economy of strokes—the moment-by-moment urgency of life itself."

Once you join a class there is an expectation of practice, regular practice. (What other kind is there?) So the next question was: When would I fit this in so that it actually got done? I decided that the evenings would be the best time since then I would not be tempted by e-mail. But evenings came and went, and I usually felt too tired for the unfamiliar discipline of holding the brush wedged between my middle and ring fingers, keeping my elbow down, pushing or pulling the brush with the whole arm, not just the fingers or wrist, and keeping my attention where the ink was flowing onto the newsprint (which is what is used to begin with). Eventually, I realized that the only way to practice is to do so when it occurs to me, immediately—not planning it for some time in the future, because that time will probably never arrive.

I know that that was rather a long story, but I wanted to trace the maneuverings of my mind over the last twenty years and illustrate the lengths to which a seemingly intelligent person will go to avoid doing the obvious. Now that I have actually started the Sumi-e painting, I feel as though I have a responsibility toward it. I practice whenever the impulse arises, and this might be in the middle of the morning, sometime in the afternoon, or in the evening. It doesn't matter, as long as it gets done. And I don't kid myself that it is going to happen absolutely every day. It gets done as often as it gets done—probably three or four times a week in addition to the two-hour lesson on the weekend. It is a tremendous relief to me that I have resolved this amicably with myself.

This approach is working with other things, too. Writing and answering e-mail *is* compulsive, but I have now given myself the freedom to get up from the computer and walk around the house when I feel like it, do a little cleaning (rather than launch a major blitz once a week), correct galleys while snuggled under a blanket on the sofa, run a few errands on Broadway, or go for a walk in the park with a friend. I have even made a date recently to go to a foreign film at lunchtime. This last sortie seemed almost sinful to me after so many years attached to my desk during the workweek, but I am learning (slowly) to relinquish the attachment to my desk.

You may be wondering what all this has to do with living a simple life. What I am endeavoring to do is abandon as many outmoded ideas that I have been harboring as I can, so that my head and heart are clearer and my step lighter. I recently attended a two-day seminar on the variety of meditation practices available from different traditions. It was given by the elderly, inimitable, Sufi teacher, Pir Vilayat Khan. I took copious notes about different states of consciousness and what needed to be done to reach them, but the deepest impression that remains with me is his instruction that we should become like gossamer. This is a wonderful image and illustrates precisely how I am trying to live these days.

Not only am I doing my best to eliminate the inessential, but I am also trying to do what is essential. Like the S-shaped duo of yin and yang, these are two aspects of the same principle. You cannot have one without the other.

THREE

How Much Is Enough?

Most people believe that they expend just the right amount of energy for whatever it is they are doing. If you are like me, however, when the phone rings not only do you try to pick it up immediately but you also grip it far harder than you need to. The verb that is generally used regarding phones is "cradle," but that is rarely what people do with them. The person at the other end is not going to give up after just a couple of rings, so you don't have to act as though the call is an emergency. When you pick up the receiver, notice how tightly you are holding it and see if you can relax. Whatever tension there is in your hand will communicate itself to the rest of your body and vice versa, because the two parts are physically connected. If you can relax the muscles in your hand, that release will be felt throughout your body. What a relief. Enlightenment begins with relaxation. The hint is right there in the word itself: *en-lighten-ment*.

Hardly anyone handles a tool with just the right amount of energy. When you want to sweep the floor, all you need is the minimum amount of energy to stop the broom from falling out of your hand. The broom does not need to be pushed or pulled across the surface of the floor. There is a natural wide and gentle movement from the shoulder, in which just the tips of the bristles whisper across the wood catching any dust and transporting it into your little pile. This is a very different activity from the one we normally engage in.

Observe what you do when you open a door. We tend to put about 100 percent more force into every movement than we need. Only a very small amount of energy is needed to turn the handle of the door and push it open. That is the way the door handle and the door hinges are designed. Experiment with actions like these to see how little force is really needed. It will be a revelation. Each time we relinquish this effort, we will be able to save strength and energy for doing something else. One of the reasons we all get so tired and run out of energy is that we usually expend far more than we need at any given moment.

Much of this added tension comes about because we are not content to simply perform actions. We add into them layers of feeling and desire that are counterproductive, and we often start off with the wrong aim, so it is a good idea to look for your intention and see if you can recognize it at the same time as you check on the level of effort you are putting into everything.

Recently I was home visiting my eighty-eight-year-old mother and discovered that everything I touched in the kitchen was grimy and greasy. As I scrubbed away I was seething over the fact that the person who was being paid to do this job on a regular basis was either lazy, unskilled, or in dire need of glasses. At times I became so concentrated on my resentment that I lost track of the cleaning.

I was already an adult when I started to learn how to play the piano, and I found it inordinately difficult. At the end of my lesson, I would be wiped out for the rest of the evening. The man I worked for at the time found this very puzzling because to him playing the piano was a real joy (and this is certainly what I had hoped for, too). I explained to him that it was draining because I made so many mistakes and I saw this as failure. I wanted so much to get it right. He pointed out to me that if I could play perfectly, I would have no more need of instruction. My teacher did not expect me to get everything right, so why should I? It was then that I realized that I had been putting my effort into the trying—trying to get the notes right. But it was misguided nonetheless. I had two desires operating. One was to perform perfectly and the other to make music. The former was stronger than the latter. I had put the cart before the horse.

If you can catch a glimpse of your desires and let go of them, then you can devote yourself completely to whatever it is you want to do so that your effort is untrammeled—which brings to mind the word *impedimenta*, the Latin for "baggage." We need to surrender any unnecessary baggage so that we can travel lightly.

This may be a rather revolutionary concept to many people in the United States, but it is worth experimenting with. When you sit down to a meal, help yourself to no more than you are certain you can eat. You can always have more; once something is on your plate, however, it tends to get thrown out if you don't finish it. I am not sure why so many of us put so much food on our plates. It can't be that we fear starvation—not in this generation and in this country. Even after almost forty years in New York City, I am uncomfortable with the amount of food restaurants serve. Meal after meal and day after day, they discard our leftovers. Has it never occurred to them that we might prefer to eat less, pay less, and weigh less?

My parents were scrupulously honest and upright, but I was always troubled by one of my mother's quirks. When she ate at restaurants that sported ashtrays with their names emblazoned on them, she would often bring one home with her. Over and over again I would say, "Darling, that's stealing."

"No, it's not," she would retort. "It's ashtrays. Restaurants expect you to take them home. This is their way of advertising." On reflection, the explanation seemed a reasonable one, but it left me with a certain degree of uneasiness.

I think there were two aspects of it that did not sit well with me. One was the principle of not taking something that doesn't belong to you and is not freely offered (the maître d' hadn't pressed an ashtray into her hands as she left). The other was that people tend to help themselves to whatever is available, even if it is something they don't need. If I remember rightly, my mother had given up smoking years earlier and so had absolutely no use for all those ashtrays. She just found the concept of free stuff irresistible.

A few weeks ago I was passing one of the new MetroCard-dispensing machines at a subway station. Out of the corner of my eye I watched a man take his card and walk away, forgetting to pick up his change. The machine kept blinking its message about the change, and the coins lay in the slot beneath. I experienced a momentary tug toward the money, but then a little voice said, "That money isn't yours. And even if the man doesn't come back to claim it, there are other people who could really use it. You don't actually need it." I admitted this was true and walked on.

Many people treat life like a smorgasbord. They pile their plates high with a huge assortment of delicacies, simply because the food or whatever is available. Their selection and the amount of it they take bear no relation to their need at the moment. I am reminded of the ad that the Archer Daniels Midland Company ran on PBS. It said that there is no shortage of food in the world: The problem is not the food; it is the politics. So the reason that there often doesn't seem to be enough of anything to go around is often a question of inappropriate appropriation or hogging it.

Some years ago I visited an old high-school friend in Washington, D.C., and she threw a party for me. Since her husband worked for the World Bank and she was connected to American University, almost all the guests moved in these circles, both of which were unfamiliar to me. Everyone I encountered seemed to be studying at night, in addition to working during the day. Eventually someone asked me what courses I was taking. I explained that I worked in publishing and so there was not any need to take courses. I found the question very puzzling.

"But if you learned something new, you could get promoted or move on to a better job," the woman said.

"You can't learn publishing in a class," I said. "You just have to plunge in and learn as you go. I have been doing this for many years, and I know how to do it. I love what I do and I don't want to do anything else or work anywhere else, so what would be the point of taking classes?" Neither of us could comprehend the other's point of view. We were like two ships passing in the night. All these people were on a restless search for something more or something else.

A slogan familiar to many people is "Less is more," and once I saw the beauty of it in operation, I espoused it completely. But lately I have begun to detect a basic fallacy in it. In this consumer society, we have been conditioned to believe that more is always better. (I once thought of getting in touch with Macy's to offer them what I thought would be the perfect advertising line: "Macy's has more.") Now I realize that I don't want more. I simply want enough. Although "Less is more" sounds as though it is a way of cutting back, of returning to simplicity, it contains the subtle message that if you have less, you will receive more. It is still a promise that more is better.

I went to Havana in 1997 and saw the conditions under which the Cubans lived because of the U.S. embargo. This was the first time I understood that "Less is more" doesn't apply to every situation. The people I met had hardly anything, but they were cheerful and not resentful. Less isn't more when you don't have very much; however, the Cubans did have just enough to keep going, and so it was enough. It is the same way with the rest of us. Less doesn't necessarily have to be more. We simply need to have whatever is sufficient to deal with the situation we find ourselves in. So I propose that we change the adage to "Less is enough." What do you think?

The whole question of why our lives seem so unsatisfying needs close examination. Why is it that our experiences or possessions never seem to bring us lasting happiness or a sense of completion? We always want something more, and it is always eluding us. Not only do we want to hold on to what we already have but we also want to acquire as much more as we can. I think of possessions as possessing me rather than vice versa. If you own something, then you are responsible for taking care of it and are continually worrying that it might get harmed or you might lose it.

We try to fill the vacuum that we believe to be inside us, but we need to remember that we didn't come into this life to shop, to chalk up experiences, to amass objects we can't take with us when we go, or even to make a lot of money.

In truth, it is not the number and diversity of our possessions that are the problems but our attachment to them. When the attachment grows thin and the fila-ment breaks, then we discover that we do not really want so much anymore. What we need to relinquish, therefore, is our attachment to possessions and experiences, not the things themselves. The freedom we are all seeking is freedom from the fear of losing what we believe we own.

Among the notes I have kept over the years is a small scrap of paper on which I typed out a passage from a book by Robert Pilpel, entitled *Between Eternities*. It speaks with extraordinary clarity on this whole matter:

> You wonder about the next life because this life's not enough for you. And this life's not enough for you because you're not living it but thinking about it.
>
> I thought that there had to be more to life than being alive and I resolved never to be satisfied with my existence until that something more, whatever it was, had been savored to the full. I felt, moreover, that once my great goal had been achieved I would be prepared to die. . . .
>
> Why are we afraid of death? Surely it is not because the process of dying is painful—because the process of living is infinitely more so. And we don't fear living—at least, not as much as we fear dying. We

are afraid to die because we are not ready. Does death stand for our final failure to achieve the unattainable? And if it does, what then does the unattainable stand for? Would I want it so much if I knew what it was?

When I think back to what I believed would be the most memorable moments in my life—confirmation, the first time I made love, my wedding ceremony, the birth of my son—I remember that each time I had expected to feel different in some way. I anticipated that something in me would be transformed forever. But nothing like that ever happened, and the next day it was always recognizably the same me who woke up in the morning.

Why is it that we yearn to be more or other than we are? It so rarely occurs to us that what we are looking for may be—indeed, always is—already within us, simply undiscovered.

At Play

If you want to know someone well, watch how she walks, talks, stands, sits, and speaks. This will reveal exactly how her mind operates. Just observing fellow travelers in the subway tells you a great deal about them without your ever being introduced. If you want to know even more about the person, watch what she does in her leisure time. Knowing that will help you understand what makes another person tick.

Take me, for example. What have I ever done in my spare time but work? Yes, occasionally, I have taken time off, but I have had to force myself to do it. I was brought up (how on earth did this begin?) to finish my work before I began to play. Of course, there is always more work and so I rarely, if ever, got around to playing.

I remember an occasion many years ago when an author and I had been working very hard for months on his book. One afternoon everything was finally done, and I said, "The work is over. Now we can play." And then we realized that neither of us even knew where or how to begin. Most of the time I still feel that way, but I am determined to make up for all the time I have lost.

I don't know whether my son is typical of the current generation, but we have always had a difference of opinion about work. I believe that you do your chores first and, if there is time left over, then you are free to play. He believes the opposite, probably because he has observed me slaving away for the last twenty-three years. All he has ever seen me do is work; perhaps he has come to the conclusion that this is no way to spend a life, so (as far as I can tell) he gets in as much play as possible first and manages to squeeze in a little work at the end.

When I consider the implications of how I have spent my life so far, I am appalled. Somehow, I have completely overlooked the importance of playing and what its significance is. Many of the sacred teachings I have studied (particularly Vedanta) go out of their way to point out that creation is one great play and that whatever or whoever produced this play did so for the sake of enjoyment—his/hers/its *and* ours. We came into this world, the current production, as players not workers. We have roles that may shift from moment to moment, depending on the director, but we don't have to write the script, paint the scenery, or sell the tickets. We just have to play our parts. Why is this something that I fail to remember over and over again? Most of the time I, and probably you too, labor under the delusion that I am responsible for all aspects of the play when the truth is that I just have to be there for the performance. And if I'm not, neither I nor the audience will enjoy it.

Perhaps this can be most clearly seen on stage. Once you have experienced it there, it is easier to put it into practice in your daily life. The most memorable performances I have witnessed were those of Mikhail Baryshnikov dancing at the New York City Ballet when he first came to the West, and Douglas Perry who sung the part of Gandhi in Philip Glass's Sanskrit opera

Satyagraha, which I saw at the Brooklyn Academy of Music. In each case, the performer was having such a good time, he positively glowed. The light was flooding out of him irrepressibly. He was enjoying himself in every sense of the word. And so we, the audience, shared his enjoyment. This is the way to go through life. And if you are wondering what all this has to do with not living to excess, here's the answer: There was an article in *Reader's Digest* umpteen years ago in which I learned that far fewer muscles are required in smiling than looking sad. Less tension is involved.

So, whether it is someone else you want to know about or yourself, have a look at what this person does when not working and also see if he or she is enjoying it. Are you spending all your time watching television (whatever the excuse)? If so, what does this say about you? Do you seem to do nothing but cook? Does he devote himself to music?

I wonder how I got to this ripe age feeling so driven by my work? Although it is not uncommon in the United States, remember that I grew up in England where to talk of how you earn a living (or religion, politics, or sex) is just not done. In this country, almost the first thing you say to someone when you meet is

"What do you do?" This is not a question that would ever be asked in the United Kingdom. Here in New York I love to talk about my work with and for authors. But when I go home, no one wants to know about it. No one asks, and so I don't tell.

My first job was in a public library. The salary was so small that by the time I got my paycheck at the end of the month, it wasn't even enough to cover my expenses although I was living at home. I cycled to work and took a sandwich for my lunch, but even these economies didn't seem to help. My time was spent stamping books and putting the volumes that had been returned back on the shelves. The high point of my day would be when someone asked me, "Can you recommend me a good book, miss?" (I would hastily scan the first and last pages of whatever I was holding at the time so that I could describe the kind of book it was) or once, "Do you have books on learning foreign languages? I'm going to Switzerland for my holidays, and I want to learn Swiss." After three months of this, I had managed to reimburse my parents for the money they had had to lend me during my time at the library. Then I quit, having discovered that the only way for advancement as a librarian was to study for the equivalent of a university degree in my spare time. This would then qualify me to choose purchases for the library from lists of books that circulated once a week and also, presumably, rule the roost over the other bluestockings who worked at the branch. The prospects were not thrilling. Surely there was more to life than that?

So I enrolled in a secretarial college for young ladies in Mayfair. In those days that meant Pitman's shorthand (I took rapid dictation in minuscule glyphs), typing at a speed of at least sixty words a minute on a manual typewriter, learning how to lay out a letter or document so that it was good enough to be framed, and commercial French, Spanish, and German. I managed to cram the year's course into six months. Then I applied for a job at the Automobile Association, where I spent six months translating the descriptions of members' cars into French for their *carnets* (passports for cars to travel in Europe). There turned out to be no future in that job, either, so I moved to the foreign franchise department of Schweppes, working for six roving managers, and from there to Pirelli (the footware, not the tire division), and then on to a chemical company, and eventually a small engineering firm in Chelsea.

Each time that I found myself in a new situation, it took me about three months to understand the business and how it functioned, and then I would revamp all the office systems to make them work more efficiently. That would take me another three months, but then there would be no further challenge. All the executives were always men, and all the secretaries young women. Even if I thought I could do the job better than most of the men, no one would ever have considered asking me to. I didn't have a degree, and I wasn't a man.

So I consulted someone about what other possibilities there might be for an intelligent woman, and he told me that there were two avenues I could pursue without a degree: advertising and publishing. In both these spheres women had already made their way, and there was no reason why I might not do the same. I had no interest in advertising and I had started out with books in the first place, so I applied for a job at André Deutsch Ltd., a small independent publishing house (they were almost all independent in those days, but they weren't all small).

Now that I think about it, I am amazed I took the job. I was interviewed and hired as André Deutsch's assistant by a young American editor who herself had just started work there. My salary was to be £12 a week rather than the £15 I was then earning (it took me three years to get back to £15), and I would not meet André himself until the following week.

I suppose that it was there that I learned to work so hard and think of almost nothing else. I shared an office with another young woman. Perhaps *office* is too dignified a word for our space. We sat side by side at the end of a corridor. Beside us on the floor was a huge pile of unopened manuscripts that we attacked once a week, carefully saving the envelopes in which they had arrived so that we could reuse them later. On the other side was another pile of manuscripts waiting to be rejected. Shirley worked for the production manager and two editors (each of these jobs was a full-time occupation). I worked for André. And between us we coped with the manuscripts that ebbed and flowed around us, confiding in each other that we thought we might be able to get everything done if it were not for the authors. But, of course, without the authors there would be nothing to publish.

André was a short, charming, distinguished-looking man from Budapest. It was common knowledge that the three most important things in his life were his work. And it was also rumored that you could trust André as far as you could throw George Weidenfeld (in those days, this physically large and successful publisher had not yet been knighted). This was both unfair and unwarranted. I worked for André for more than three years, and I never caught him doing anything illegal or even unethical. He made sure that he always received whatever he was entitled to in full measure but that was as far as it went. When it was clear that paying a bill could no longer be avoided, he would instruct the business manager to send a check to the American publisher "by fast sea mail" (perhaps he thought that the post office used ships that traveled at two different speeds?).

He would appear at our end of the corridor just as we were about to leave for the day, with his shirtsleeves rolled up and a letter that had to be dictated immediately. And he would stand just behind one of us, almost touching but not quite, until the letter was finished. He had enormous animal magnetism, and he used it. He knew that there was no way we were strong enough to refuse to stay late if he flashed his smile. By the time each of us had taken the train home, it would be late and we would be so exhausted that we would often cry over our supper.

I wondered how to extricate myself from this situation, and then the young woman who handled the foreign rights decided to leave, so I asked if I could take on her job. André was willing for me to do so but insisted that I continue as his secretary as well. I asked to be paid more if I was going to take on the additional work, and he said no: If I wanted the job, I could have it. If not, that was fine too. In retrospect, I see that this was blackmail. He would have had to pay someone else to handle foreign rights if I had not shouldered the responsibility. But I suppose he reckoned that it was a good gamble, and he won. I agreed to do the extra work without remuneration so that I could learn a new skill and move to a better job elsewhere.

André was a hard taskmaster, but I learned a lot from him. He knew how to sell anything. Anything. It just so happened that he had ended up as a publisher, but he would probably have been equally successful in another business. I noticed that he hardly ever named a price himself. If he was selling the translation rights to a book, he invited the other publisher to make an offer and then insisted that the figure was too low, no matter how much money was involved. This was a very neat trick. I suppose that occasionally he must have been put in a situation where he needed to name a sum himself but, if I remember rightly, he would then ask for something preposterous so that the other publisher would be forced to offer more than he had originally anticipated.

A year or so after I had taken on the second job I went to the United States for a month's vacation. It wasn't that this was somewhere I had yearned to visit, but a Pakistani friend from high school (the one who threw a party for me many years later in Washington, D.C.) was now living in upstate New York and had sent me a Christmas card asking when I was coming to visit. My mother said, "Why not?" and so that spring I went.

Later that year I spotted on André's calendar that Bob Gottlieb, then managing editor at Simon and Schuster, was coming to see him. About ten minutes into the appointment, André's phone rang, he picked it up, and then stayed on the phone for an unconscionably long time. I had grown used to this behavior, and I knew how much New York editors fretted at being kept waiting when they had half a dozen more appointments to get to later in the day. I stopped what I was doing, slipped into the room, sat down next to the visitor, and said, "You must be Bob Gottlieb. My name is Toinette Rees. We met earlier this year when I went to New York. How is Jean?"

Jean Jollett was Bob's assistant, and I had had an introduction to her from an editor at Deutsch who had recently returned from an eighteen-month stint working for Bob. I had really enjoyed the time I had spent with Jean, and so I asked Bob whether there was a chance of her coming to London on some kind of working vacation.

"Oh, no," he said. "Actually, my editorial assistant has just left, and I'm promoting Jean to this position. If you want to see Jean, you'll have to come to New York."

"In publishing it takes a lifetime to save enough to go to America," I replied. "I did save and I went but now I would have to save for another lifetime. I couldn't come unless I had a job." I was just chatting idly in the hope that André would be courteous enough to get off the phone soon and let me get back to what I had been doing.

"Well," said Bob. "Why don't you come and work for me? I need a new assistant."

I was dumbfounded. "But you don't even know me," I said. I'd spoken to him for about three minutes one day after I had had lunch with Jean in New York. I don't think I would have recognized him in the street. He looked like a tall Woody Allen, but at that time I had never heard of Woody Allen. This was, after all, September 1964.

"No, but Jean knows you and likes you and that's good enough for me," he responded. "Can you type?"

"Of course, I can type," I said. "Why do you ask?"

"Because I want to make sure that you are a good typist."

"If I come, may I come just for a year?" I asked. I had recently explored the possibilities of getting a job selling rights in other London publishing houses. There were only three houses that I really wanted to work for, and none of them had a vacancy at that time. It occurred to me that if I went away for a year and got more experience, I could come back and perhaps command a better position. After all, the chief editor at Deutsch had got her job after working as Bob's assistant. Bob, who had achieved fame as the editor of

Joseph Heller's *Catch-22,* had the reputation of being the best young editor in the English-speaking world.

"I want someone forever," he replied.

"But you might not live that long," I pointed out.

"No, I might crash on the way home on Sunday and then you wouldn't even get the job." It transpired that he was terrified of flying and always crossed the Atlantic by boat. This would be the first time he had boarded a plane.

"Well, if you don't crash and I do come, may I come just for a year? And how much would you pay?"

"I believe we pay new assistants ninety dollars a week, but in any case I would need to check with my colleagues," he said.

"I'm not a beginner. I have been working for seven years and have been working for André for more than three. When I was in New York, I was told that a British secretary could earn one hundred and twenty dollars a week."

"Not in publishing," Bob replied.

"You begin to sound like André already," I retorted. "Why don't you go back and find out how much you could pay me, then write me a letter offering me a job in your editorial department reading French and

German novels. I promise you I won't take you up on that, since I don't like French and German novels even though I speak both languages. It wouldn't be worth your while to ask me to read them because I would always write negative reports. But there's currently an embargo on British secretaries in New York City (where on earth could I have picked up this snippet of information?), so if I am going to get a visa, I'll need evidence that I have a job offer for something else. It takes six weeks to get an American visa (again, I wonder how I knew this) and five days to cross the Atlantic in a boat. If I am bringing my belongings for a year, I won't be able to fly. So I could be with you about seven weeks after I got your offer."

On reflection, this was a very saucy way of responding to a prospective employer, but at the time I believed that I was just doing my best to distract a visiting American editor. I wasn't taking the conversation seriously in any way. But suddenly everything shifted.

Before Bob could respond to my proposition, André finally hung up the phone. What I haven't yet mentioned is why he had remained on this call for so long. He was inordinately proud of the fact that he had published *The Magic Christian* and *Flash and Filigree* by the

American novelist Terry Southern before they had appeared in the United States. Then Terry had written *Candy*, which had been published anonymously as *Lollipop* in Paris by Maurice Girodias at Olympia Press. André had just heard that the book was being published in America by Grove Press, and he wanted to publish it in the U.K. But André was a Hungarian Jew who had come to England at the beginning of World War II, and he didn't want to risk going to prison. Much as he hated to give up any potential profit, he was trying to persuade two other editors to copublish the book with him. He believed that, although the director of public prosecutions might send one publisher to prison for obscenity, it was unlikely that he would send three. André had already got the relatively new young publisher, Anthony Blond, to come in with him, and he had spent the last twenty minutes trying to persuade the much older and very distinguished Fred Warburg of Secker & Warburg to do the same. Fred had been arguing that he didn't believe that *Candy* was a satire on pornography. As far as he was concerned, it was simply pornography. And he didn't think it was particularly well written. He was not willing to publish the book at all. André never achieved his goal. In the end it was published in London many years later by John Calder.

"Can this girl type?" Bob asked.

"Of course she can type. Why do you ask?" André replied.

"Because she is going to come and be my secretary," Bob announced. This was news to me, but I didn't say anything. I thought I had just been distracting a nice American editor while my employer was being rude.

"What about me?" asked André.

"You are welcome to come and be my secretary if you like, but you probably wouldn't want to for a hundred dollars a week," said Bob.

"So what would I get in return?"

"What would you like?" responded Bob. (I began to feel like merchandise being haggled over. For the moment, both men seemed to have forgotten that I was still in the room.)

"Well, I will want a lot of titles," said André, always having the profit motive in mind. What he meant was that he expected Bob to give him an exclusive look at a large number of Simon and Schuster books that he might purchase for publication in the U.K.

"You mean after all these years all you want in exchange for Toinette is some books?" Bob and I looked directly at each other (only at that moment did all this suddenly become real for me) and then at André.

André saw that he had made a grave error. "Oh, I didn't mean that," he said, but, of course, he did.

The next thing I remember was boarding the SS *France* for an exceedingly tempestuous voyage across the Atlantic Ocean. I was twenty-five years old when I arrived in New York on November 10, 1964, and I started work at Simon and Schuster the next day.

I was so accustomed to having far more to do than was physically possible that each day I soon finished everything that Bob gave me. I don't think he was used to someone who worked with such intensity. He found my empty desk a reproach, and when I asked for more to do, his response was, "We don't pay you to work here. We pay you to be here." It is interesting that he put it like this. I have told this story many times in my life, but only now do I grasp the full significance of what he was saying. Being present (and knowing it) is one of the most important things that one can do in life, while work can be achieved without complete presence. (Perhaps the work itself will not be perfect but most people won't spot the difference.)

Shortly after I arrived in New York, I went to live in an apartment on the Upper West Side with two young women who also worked in publishing and one and a half Siamese cats (one was only half Siamese). I had thought that I would be better off sharing with others in a strange city where I had no friends, but the cats were always trying to climb the net curtains and they were very vocal. I soon realized that what I really wanted was to be on my own.

Then, after three months, a dear little apartment fell into my lap, but not in a way that made me happy. I had come to New York to work for a brilliant editor and to improve my chances of getting the job I wanted on my return to London, but I had also come because I wanted to spend time with Jean, whom I had really enjoyed meeting on my earlier visit. When I arrived back in New York, I found that Jean was in the throes of a romance. She had little time for me and soon decided to get married and leave Simon and Schuster. She bequeathed to me her six-floor walkup apartment on East Seventh Street between Second and Third avenues, a few steps from Cooper Union. For $300 key money I inherited the contents of the apartment. (It included everything I could possibly need, plus a large library of paperback books. All she took with her was her coffee pot.) And the rent was only $37.24 a month—a steal even in those days.

From my kitchen window I had a view of the green-blue onion domes of the Ukrainian Orthodox church next door (alas, this lovely little church was pulled down to make way for the large new brick edifice for which the congregation was saving in the early sixties). This was a time of flux in the East Village. For years it had been the Ukrainian section of the city, but during the three years I lived there the face of the neighborhood changed almost unrecognizably. There had always been old bums drifting over from the Bowery in a drunken stupor, but now young panhandlers appeared asking for money to support their drug habits. I felt sorry for the old-timers, even though I didn't give them any donations for liquor. I would smile and shake my head and they would generally say, "God bless you anyway, lady." But I saw absolutely no reason why the nineteen-year-olds should expect the world to help them out.

When I moved in, friends advised me to take a taxi home if I was ever out alone after dark, so that no one would follow me into the tenement building. But time and again I would huff and puff my way up the six flights of stairs and collapse onto the bed, only to realize that I had once more forgotten to take a cab.

As the year wore on, people would ask me whether I really planned to return to London in November. I would look at Bob, he would look at me, and neither of us would say anything. The more I considered it, the more ridiculous it seemed for me to go back to England at the end of my year simply because I had said I would. I had no job offer, no place to live, and no pressing relationship to return to. I stayed. Bob never said anything, but several years passed and I thoroughly enjoyed my work with him. There was always something new to learn—manuscripts to read, authors to meet, books to edit, jacket copy to write. We all used to joke that working at S&S was like having an extra family you didn't need. If you were out sick one day, three or four people would call to find out what had happened and what they could do to help. I had never been part of a community like that before.

We all have different experiences at work, whether

we are employed in a large organization or a small company or whether we work on our own. But the one thing that we share is the belief that the results of the work belong to us. It goes further than taking pride in our work. We put a claim on it. We are convinced that what we have produced bears our mark, that we deserve recognition, remuneration, advancement, whatever. But here is the truth about the situation:

> All that lives is full of the Lord. Claim nothing; enjoy. Do not covet His property. Then hope for a hundred years of life doing your duty. No other way can prevent deeds from clinging, proud as you are of your human life.

For me, this quotation from the beginning of the three-thousand-year-old *Isha Upanishad* is one of the most powerful teachings I have ever encountered. It goes so much further than Jesus' teaching "Render unto Caesar the things that are Caesar's and unto God the things that are God's." It tells us that everything, no matter what it is, belongs to God, that it is all His property, that we cannot claim any of it. It also instructs us to enjoy the creation. This is a commandment, one that we fail to keep most of the time. The text doesn't say: "Try to enjoy things." It just says, "Enjoy." This view of work is similar to that taken in the *Bhagavad Gita*, where a great deal is said about actions, who does them, and who is entitled to the results. There Krishna declares to Arjuna that we have "only the right to work but none to the fruit thereof," and he urges him not to let the fruit be the motive for work, as it is for so many of us.

Some people may find this view difficult to accept. Surely, if we work hard and do a good job, we should be entitled to something? As Eartha Kitt used to sing, "If I can't take it with me when I go, I just ain't gonna go." But even she has no choice. Better to admit that we don't really own anything, that none of it—possessions, cash, reputation, know-how—is going with us on our journey into the beyond. We can have fun doing things, but the experience is fleeting. We can take delight in the results, but we can't say that we own them in any way. Once we admit this, a huge burden is lifted from our backs.

FIVE

Nothing Unnecessary

Some years ago I was invited to attend a conference on inner science at which His Holiness the Fourteenth Dalai Lama spoke. I listened to him elucidating Buddhist dialectics for three days and was for the most part unable to understand the content or direction of his argument; however, I soon became aware that his actual teaching—at least for me—was going on at another level. I noticed that whatever he did or said, he did with his whole being—whether it was laughing, talking, or just resting. Part of him was not doing something else. He was completely concentrated in the moment, and the power of his unsplintered attention was electrifying. Not only was all his attention given to whatever he chose, but mine was also. Since he was not distracted, neither was I. I left the conference in some amazement, never before (or since) having met anyone who appeared able to focus in this way. This teaching was a tremendous gift.

This morning I heard from an old colleague musing in a wistful tone about when he could retire from his job and just do one thing at a time. He felt completely overwhelmed and torn apart by the multitude of tasks in front of him. The truth is, you don't have to wait for retirement to do only one thing at a time. There really isn't any other way to do things. People who believe that they can do more than one thing at a time are just fooling themselves. If you split your attention among, say, three jobs, all you are doing is giving your attention to one of them, then leaving that one for a minute and moving to the next, and so on. I know it looks and feels as though you are doing everything at the same time, but look again.

Most of us are brought up to believe that it is advantageous to do as many things as possible at the same time; however, if we observe carefully, we will discover that this is not only undesirable but also counterproductive. Unfortunately, we not only believe that doing more than one thing at a time is good, but we have also drawn a veil over our activities so that for the most part we are oblivious to what is actually happening.

Take ironing, for example. You may remain aware of what you are doing while you are laying the garment on the ironing board. As soon as your hand begins to steer the iron over the garment, however, your thoughts are off and away. Ironing is one of the dreamiest activities. It is a useful exercise to give full attention to the ironing and see if you can spot the mind's tendency to wander off. Each time it does, gently bring it back to the task at hand. The ironing will be accomplished better and in less time if it is done without the mind doing something else. In addition, you will discover that ironing—or anything else, for that matter—is not a boring activity. Usually, what makes something appear boring is that we are not giving it any attention. When we give it our undivided attention, many details become clear—things that we would ordinarily miss— and the result may be intriguing.

Obviously, we can walk along the street *and* look into store windows as we pass them. However, we can give our attention to only one of these activities. If the walking is going along fine by itself, it is easy to look in a window. Yet, if we stumble, knock into someone, or hear a screech of brakes, our attention immediately leaves the store window and is drawn to whatever requires it. It goes there instantly, and the window is forgotten. Most of us walk down the street with our attention neither on the activity of walking nor on the windows of the stores we are passing; not on the architecture of the buildings or on the behavior of the drivers a few feet from us; not on the clouds or planes in the sky, and probably not often on the people walking alongside us or approaching us. We are simply lost in thought, rehearsing something that happened and we wish it hadn't, or something that we would like to happen, going through a mental checklist of things that need doing or people we hope to see—anything but giving attention to where we are and what is taking place. These mental conversations that we have with ourselves are generally not very fruitful because we cannot rewrite history, and if we are scripting a future conversation, the chances are that other people will not be aware of their cues when the time comes. And while this energy-consuming activity is taking place in our heads, the world is turning and we are missing so much that is taking place. It seems sad not to embrace the fullness of the moment in which anything may be revealed.

I once attended a press conference and watched the reporters scribbling furiously (it was in the days before people used tape recorders to do their work for them). Then I noticed one man sitting very still and not taking notes. He just listened. Afterward I asked him why he had not written anything down, and he replied that if he took notes, he would be doing two things at a time and would therefore undoubtedly miss something. He did not wish to split his attention.

I was thinking about this recently, in particular with regard to studying and learning, because our training has been to take notes on everything we are taught in school so that we can refer back to them later, and I wondered why we all do this. When we read an item in a book or newspaper, hear about an event, or discover an idea by ourselves, we have no difficulty whatever remembering it and reporting it afterward. This is because it is something that interests us, something that caught and held our attention. The trouble comes only when we are not interested in something:

for instance, if we are taking a course and need to study something that is required and we wish it weren't. What happens then is that we tend to focus on our resistance to the matter at hand rather than whatever it is we are supposed to be learning. So the secret is to be interested in whatever we are learning or doing. Then the full power of our consciousness flows to it, it goes directly into the mind, and we have no difficulty retrieving it later. It does not have to be "learned." The learning happens naturally.

Until a short time ago, while I was still working in a big office, I would be sitting at my desk typing away when the phone would ring and I would answer it immediately. Before I could get back to what I was doing, someone would walk into my office to discuss something he or she felt was much more important than whatever I might be doing. Then I would check my e-mail to make sure that I wasn't missing anything. After I'd fired off three e-mails and answered the phone again and made a note to myself of something I had planned to do first thing in the day, I would remember that I had been in the middle of typing a letter about half an hour earlier. This is the way our lives tend to run. Even now that I work at home, it is no different. Yes, it would be wonderful if there were no interruptions, but even if you are alone with no phone and no e-mail, there are still your thoughts to distract you.

There is a way to approach your work that takes all this into account. Usually while this maelstrom of distractions is taking place, we are dragged from one demand to another, trailing our attention behind us. By which I mean that we don't relinquish whatever we are doing when we are interrupted. You need to make a clean break. Just drop whatever it is. That way you are doing only one thing at a time, even if it is in small drafts. Carrying your regrets about not finishing the first task into the second and then the third is counterproductive. We have enough to do these days without bearing this extra weight. The important thing is to come to each job fresh, as though it were the only thing in the world. When the right moment comes, you will get back to the first task. Good luck.

Postscript: A few days after I wrote the last paragraph, I was cheerfully answering e-mail, dreaming up fact sheets on next fall's books for the sales force, receiving a fax, and trying to write some of my own book. I thought I had all my balls in the air, and then something stalled in the computer system, the screen froze, and my options dwindled down to shutting off the computer or shutting off the computer. Alack and alas, the copy I had concocted for one of the fall books dematerialized because I hadn't saved it. The lesson to be learned from this, I suppose, is that it is okay to shift your attention from one job to another, but you must make sure that everything is in good order before you do so, whether this means putting the saw out of harm's way so that no one will trip over it or turning off the flame under the pan of milk before you leave the kitchen. One moment's inattention can cause a lot of heartache. Now to reconstruct that brilliant description that went the way of all flesh . . .

It is always important to be aware of what is going on in our minds because whatever it is, it is absorbing our energy and attention. We are giving ourselves to it. This constant activity of which most of us are completely unaware can be exhausting and wasteful of our resources. Whatever we give our attention to grows, so we should know what that is. It may be fear, loneliness, anxiety, or any number of things, but it behooves us to take a look. If what we had planned to do was take a walk, why not just walk? It could be fun, but if all we are doing is continuing an inner conversation that has been going on all day, the walk will not prove very refreshing.

Nowadays people tend to look for distraction, any distraction that will take their mind off whatever they don't want to think about. This tends to take the form of "entertainment." People will do almost anything in order to avoid being where they are, doing whatever it is that needs to be done. Sometimes they are seduced (by themselves) into thinking that whatever anyone else is doing is bound to be more interesting than what they are doing. This assumes many guises, but all of them make us restless and discontent, unable to settle down to what we really need to do, and usually unable to enjoy it.

There is one small rule that can be of enormous benefit to us not only when we are engaged in work but also throughout our lives, and it is this: Do and say nothing unnecessary. In order to observe this rule, we need to remain in the present or we will not be able to tell if something is necessary, so right from the start it can be seen that this is a useful thing to do. This maxim also implies that we will do whatever is necessary to accomplish the task at hand, while giving up what is not germane.

One of the places where it is important to recognize what is necessary and what isn't is in our own homes. I remember reading a proposal for a book about this many, many years ago. It suggested that you sit down and make a list of the things that you actually do at home most of the time and then plan your furniture and its arrangement around them. It pointed out that many people buy a three-piece suite simply because they believe it is the thing to do. But how many people actually sit on a sofa at any given time? Usually one. People feel a little crowded if they have to share a sofa with someone else. So in my living room I have two small love seats rather than one big sofa. Love seats are more intimate and more practical. I like to put my legs up when I read, so I have love seats with firm, straight backs to support me, and when I have guests, I encourage them to take their shoes off and put their legs up just the way I do.

I am lucky enough to have an eat-in kitchen with a round table and two rush-seated chairs. Because I generally avoid giving dinner parties and prefer to invite only one person at a time for a meal, I rarely use the dining room table, so I've relegated this to the far end of my living room. Luckily it is one of those tables with fold-down leaves, so it takes up very little room when it is not being used.

Every morning I do half an hour's yoga in ten minutes (this is New York, the world capital of fast living) and twenty minutes of meditation. I therefore keep my huge carpet free of furniture so that there is plenty of space for these two activities. I don't want to feel closed in or cramped for either one.

In the bedroom I have very little except a double bed low on the floor, a small bedside table with lamp, clock, coaster for my nighttime glass of water, cough lozenges (just in case), pad of paper, and pen. Over by the window there are a ficus tree and a collection of prayer plants nestling next to a couple of African baskets filled with sweaters I don't often wear. A plain rosewood chest of drawers, a standing lamp, a love seat for draping my clothes on when I undress, and a thick, cream carpet to welcome my toes when I get out of bed in the morning. On the wall above the chest is a rack for earrings so that I can see everything at a glance, and beside it an almost floor-length mirror. All the hanging clothes are hidden away in the wall closet (shirts on one side, pants in the middle, dresses and skirts on the other side). I have to admit that there is also a spinning wheel that I haven't used in twenty-five years plus two baskets of fleece, spindles, and carders. I can't bear the thought of surrendering these non-necessities that I plan to incorporate back into my life one day. It's the exception that proves the rule.

What each person needs in a particular room of the house will differ, but the trick is not to take into that room anything that isn't really necessary. "Necessary" will, of course, include beautiful things and not just useful ones, but the fewer of (each of) these there are, the better. Avoid clutter of all kinds.

About clothes: Do not be tempted to decide what you are going to wear tomorrow today. For years I would take out of my closet whatever I thought would be appropriate for the next day before I went to bed each night, under the illusion that it would save me time in the morning. To begin with, you have no idea what the weather will be like tomorrow. How reliable is the weather forecast? Yes, it may rain tomorrow, but when and where are always a mystery. More important is the fact that emotional weather also changes. There are some days when I dress in pastel shades. On others I gravitate toward browns and rusts, and so on. For some years I would arrive in the office each day and find to my astonishment that one of the production editors was attired in exactly the same colors, even though we were not close friends. Something in us was resonating. On the rare occasion when I was wearing red and she was wearing blue, we would joke about it. So the thing to do is go to the closet first thing in the morning with no fixed idea in mind and see which garments call to you. That way you will be in tune with the day and you won't have to put away a whole other set of clothes that you took out the night before but just don't seem right now.

When I was still working at Knopf, I used to receive a flood of free books, some of which we published and some of which were gifts. Still, I tried to take home only those books that I truly believed I would read. The others I returned to their donors or found other willing recipients for. And, once I have read a book, if I think that I will never reread it or refer to it again, I find someone else who would enjoy it.

I endeavor to do the same thing with my clothes. I go through my closet periodically and try to be honest with myself. If I haven't worn something in the last year, the chances are I won't wear it in the next year either. So I either find a friend who would like it or give it to a thrift store or emergency relief. I suspect that dwelling in Manhattan makes it easier to live this way because of the paucity of storage space. Most city dwellers have a hard enough time finding a home for the things they use every day. Still, it is remarkable the objects that creep into your apartment. I currently have an old phone I am kidding myself I might need if both of my current phones stopped functioning at the same time. I also have a microwave oven my son hardly used at college. I have never used a microwave and hope to go to my grave without doing so, but I have not yet managed to bring myself to take it across the street to the Salvation Army. Perhaps someone I know would welcome it?

Not introducing unwanted possessions into your home and/or surrendering those that are not being used creates not just physical space but also psychological space. People often comment on how empty my apartment is, and I think this is because it feels free and clear. There is very little in it (apart from the phone and the microwave) that is just gathering dust.

One major thing I don't bring into the house is the newspaper. Six weeks after I started work at Knopf, there was a big piece in *The New York Times* about the circumstances of Bob Gottlieb's hiring. I was shocked not by what was included in the article but what was not. The major facts had been left out; therefore, the whole report was skewed and, it seemed, malicious. This was an event that I knew about. Thereafter, I hesitated to read accounts in the newspaper of things of which I had no prior knowledge because I wouldn't know what to add in to make the picture accurate. I stopped reading the *Times,* and people continue to be amazed by this. As someone said to me the other day, "Not buying *The New York Times* represents a level of simple living far beyond anything I've considered." It's not that I am completely uninformed; I do listen to the news on the radio in the morning and watch it on television at night. And there are always friends who press upon me clippings that they have saved. But can you imagine the time, money, and energy I have saved over the last thirty-two years?

When I leave town for any reason, I have got into the habit of surrendering my apartment to a friend or an acquaintance. I don't go out and look for anyone.

What happens is that a week or so before I am leaving, I hear from someone who is hoping to find accommodation for a short period. Sometimes it is a person I know well, but often it is someone I know only by reputation. I don't charge rent. I am just happy that the space is being occupied and enjoyed. And I like the idea of someone being there in my absence to deal with any emergencies that might arise (but don't). In a way, it is odd to have guests I can't entertain personally, but I believe that they appreciate what my little home has to offer, and they will return to share it with me sometime in the future. I am also always touched by the gifts I find on my return: a bowl of tall white narcissus, a loaf of crusty bread, a new brush for the toilet— whatever the visitor perceives is *my* need.

As I was walking home along Broadway today, I saw a sign outside the corner store announcing that it was closing and that most of the merchandise was being sold at 30 percent discount. I was on my way to "my" Korean store to buy butter, but it occurred to me that the reason the store was closing was perhaps because it was in financial difficulty and I might be able to make a small contribution by purchasing anything I needed there rather than where I usually go. So I bought the butter (which wasn't reduced), plus some dried cranberries, and a jar of artichoke hearts (okay, I'll admit I also bought two bars of Toblerone because I've been experiencing a recurring desire for chocolate). I looked around at the array of other foodstuffs, but the truth is: I didn't really need anything else. For a moment I was torn between wanting to save money and realizing that there wasn't anything else in the store that I was likely to use in the next year or so, so I wouldn't really be saving any money if I bought other things. The things I purchased are things I will definitely eat over the next few weeks. I emerged unscathed, happy that I had saved a little money of my own and contributed to their cash flow while avoiding the trap of tying up my money in unnecessary goods.

All this talk of what is unnecessary raises the question: What *is* necessary? A very big question. I once gave a talk to the twelfth grade of my son's school, and the teacher who introduced me asked how I would describe the kind of books I published. "Necessary books," I replied. "I have to believe that the world really needs a book before I will take it on." This caused him to ask me to write an essay for the school magazine on "What Constitutes a Necessary Book?"

At the time (1985), I consulted my dictionary and discovered that *necessary* was defined as "needed for the continuing existence or functioning of something; essential; indispensable," and to those definitions I added "useful; a tool." On reflection, I realized that what I try to do is supply readers with something vital to body, mind, or heart, and what I see as my function is to supply this something in its most appropriate form to all those who really need it. When someone picks up a book, the title and subtitle, the color and design of the jacket, the copy on the flaps, the choice of typeface and interior design, the paper, and the binding should all inform the prospective reader of the writer's intent. I believe that the physical aspect of each book should be a reflection of everything that is within it. Because I am writing this in 2001, I must add one more thing: In publishing during the 1980s all you had to do was produce the book and float it out into the bookstores where it would find a ready audience. Now that so many more books are published each year by companies large and small and even by individuals, it is no longer enough to manufacture books; you also have to find a way of bringing them to the attention of customers, which is a much more difficult proposition.

But if you cannot do this, your books will have no chance in the marketplace, and all your effort will have been for naught.

The principle behind all this is not to waste precious energy where it is not needed. We do tend to fritter it away if we are not aware of what we are doing. Sometimes this takes the form of a nervous tapping of the foot or drumming of the fingers. I notice that television cameras often focus on people's hands and what they are doing while they are making speeches or testifying, so I am not the only person who has spotted this. I catch myself walking down the street with my hands clasped in front of me. Usually I am walking in order to get some exercise, and the best way to achieve this is not to restrict the body in any way. Let the arms swing. I don't know how I started this unfortunate habit, which creates tension rather than relaxation and has the opposite effect from the one I am hoping for, but perhaps by keeping an eye on it now, I will be able to let go enough to just walk and not clutch.

There is one thing I must record here because it was the impetus for this book: When Joel suggested that I write this book, I asked him what would be in it, and he said, "Well, when you go to make yourself a cup of tea, *you* just boil one cup of water." "Doesn't everyone?" I responded. "Of course not," he said. "Well, then, they are wasting not only water but time and energy too." He smiled and nodded. Since then I have spoken to quite a few people about this. It turns out that I am not the only person who fills the kettle with exactly the amount of water I need, but there are enough people who have never even given it a thought for me to tuck this advice into the book. Small note: It's not that I measure the water in the kettle exactly, but from years of experience I know how heavy the kettle feels when it has enough water in it for one person.

The other day I went to visit a friend with two small children. After an hour, I had had enough and was about to leave when I realized that this had been a very small respite in her day. It was possible for me to offer something I had completely overlooked. She was exhausted but hadn't mentioned it, so I asked if she would like to take a nap while I entertained the small boy (the baby was already asleep). I had been so caught up with my own agenda (did you know that this Latin word means "doing"?) that I hadn't spotted how depleted she was.

Asking yourself what is truly necessary can make an enormous difference in your life. Ask it in all kinds of circumstances—when you are tempted to criticize or gossip but also when whoever you are with is silently crying out for something and you are not noticing it because you are filled with your own thoughts.

SIX

Do It Now

In the late spring of 1999 I attended the World Sacred Music Festival in Fes. On our first full day we set off on a tour of the city (which, according to the guide, was "the third crowdiest city in Morocco") and then entered the medina—the old walled city of Fes el Bali, bustling with markets and life. It is reminiscent of the souks in the old city of Jerusalem but on a scale that is breathtaking. There are fourteen gates to this medina, and the narrow, labyrinthine passageways (there are said to be a thousand blind alleys) afford no access to cars or bicycles, so people go about on foot, and merchandise is transported on the backs of donkeys and mules that make their way hither and yon at an alarming pace. On their backs or in panniers on either side are huge loads. The men or boys who lead them or are perched on top of the packages yell out to warn everyone to get out of the way, and people flatten themselves sideways or get trampled underfoot. This is no place to become drowsy. Visitors are advised not to wander around on their own because even Fasis (inhabitants of Fes) get lost sometimes. I don't know how large the medina is, but I was told that it would take a whole hour to walk from one side to the other. Inside the medina are not just booths but workshops of every craft, *medersas* (koranic schools), mosques (there are said to be 785 in the whole of Fes, and 360 of them are in the medina), dozens of palaces, fountains, and many-chambered restaurants. And, of course, thousands of residents.

We were taken to a carpet shop that had once been a koranic school. It had very high ceilings and intricately carved white pillars, with carpets hanging on all the walls. The building was so high that there was room for three carpets, one above the other. First we gathered in the central area and were offered the proverbial mint tea. We were treated to a display of rugs from different parts of the country, made by various tribes. Two men would unroll each rug with a flourish as the third man described what we were looking at. The weavers use natural dyes: saffron for yellow, bougainvillea for peach, indigo for blue, poppy for red, and mint for green. Afterward we were led away to individual nooks where more tea was served and we were pressured by a salesman into buying whatever our hearts desired.

I certainly had no intention of buying a carpet, but within twenty minutes I found myself settling on a magnificent thick cream Berber rug with a traditional design. I picked the colors of the decoration and before long was signing away my money. A lot of haggling went on, both about whether the insurance was included in the price of shipping (as had been quoted to me) and whether they were going to charge me an extra 6 percent for using a MasterCard (I refused). The carpet would either arrive in "four to five months," or I would learn the hard way not to trust carpet salesmen. The guide who took us there (and who gets an enormous cut of the profits) said that he guaranteed I would receive it, and I certainly had his name and address if something should go wrong, but he lived a long way away and I could hardly go around to complain. Five months later the carpet did arrive at my apartment on the Upper West Side of Manhattan. It was rolled up and sewn beautifully into a protective sheath. Not only was it a miracle that it was finally there, but it also turned out to be bigger (the difference between meters and inches had been beyond my ability to calculate) and thicker than I had anticipated.

That was almost a year ago, and I have received untold pleasure from the carpet just by gazing at it and squishing my toes into it when I get out of bed in the morning—until two days ago, when I walked into the room and detected some movement out of the corner of my eye. I walked over and saw that there was a cluster of small brown moths fluttering just above it. All my good Buddhist intentions about not taking life fled. I began to pounce on the moths and speed them onto the next life by grinding them between my thumb and forefinger. They didn't put up much resistance. When I could see no more activity, I retired to the kitchen to ponder what I should do. Where there was one moth, there was always the possibility of future moths. Later in the day, I found several more on another corner of the carpet and dispatched those to kingdom come also.

I went out to the hardware store searching for a solution. There were "old-fashioned" mothballs (I bought a box of these) and a can of lethal spray (which I decided might kill me as well as the moths, so I left it in the store). I took the mothballs home and read the directions. It seemed that these too were hazardous to your health, and I worried about sleeping a few inches away from them. So I deposited the unopened box on top of the place where I had found the first colony of moths and hoped that the fierce smell emanating from it would be sufficient to deter any more eggs from hatching. Yes, I know that this wasn't a very reasonable attitude, but the instructions on the box said to place the "garment" with the mothballs inside a sealed container. Since my "garment" was larger than any container I owned, I wasn't sure how to proceed. Also, my friends were all urging me to call a carpet cleaner instantly and have the problem solved professionally. My experience with carpet cleaners (I have employed two in the past) has not been good, and I couldn't bring myself to heed this advice. You see: My luscious rug has a one-and-a-half-inch pile. It is really fluffy and shaggy, and I was afraid of what else the carpet cleaners might do to it when they deinfested it. It might never be the same rug again (as had happened when I had called in the cleaners before. Since then I bought a carpet-cleaning machine and do the work myself).

When I got up this morning I decided to take things into my own hands and see if I could effect a cure. First I vacuumed the carpet as thoroughly as I could. Then I took a stiff-bristled brush and, with the aid of my fingers, raked the pile as deeply as possible, skimming off handfuls of loose fluff. I vacuumed again. Then something made me turn over a corner of the carpet and inspect the other side. There, to my horror, was a host of tiny white eggs clinging to the back of the carpet. More brushing and vacuuming ensued. I repaired to the other site where I had found errant moths, and there were more eggs. Eventually I rolled back the entire rug and brushed until I could detect no more small white specks. Actually, I didn't find any more, but I decided to brush and beat the rug as much as I could in case some of them had been laid a little farther from the original site.

As I was clearing up, a vivid memory popped into my mind: The day I had unfurled the carpet and laid it lovingly on the floor, it had occurred to me that perhaps I should brush and clean the underside before I put it down, but then I had ignored that little warning voice. And I had paid for my "ignorance," perhaps not in spades but certainly in moths.

There have been far too many times in my life when I have ignored that voice, and I don't know why I keep doing it. There are also plenty of times when I have obeyed it, so why don't I do this all the time? It is obvious that it is better to get something right at the beginning than undo a mistake further along in the process. We know this deep down inside, but then there is our rational mind that tells us that the information being supplied by our sixth sense is "unreasonable." Believe me, it is not. If it occurs to you to do something now, just do it. Once it is done, then the weight of it, the responsibility, is released. When you see that something needs to be done, the energy to do it arises at the same moment. The longer you put off doing it, the more that energy is dissipated and the larger the task appears to be. Eventually, a task can loom so large you are unable to contemplate it. The thing to spot in all this is that it is all the extraneous thoughts that crowd into the mind unnoticed that obscure what needs to be done. These trains of thought naturally carry us away.

Trains of thought, like any other trains, are designed to carry us to destinations that are anywhere but here.

Which brings me to a mini-law that has governed my life for many years. In Sanskrit these mini-laws are known as *sutras*, short, pithy sentences that embody the essence of a universal law. Here is how this one was presented to me: "Step by step, at every step, there is that which is conducive to each step," but you could also translate it as "Whatever you need is right here." This applies not only to the energy necessary to complete a job but also, often, to the wherewithal to do it.

So much of our time is taken up in worrying about how we are going to cope with things that have not happened yet and may indeed never happen. At every moment things shift, so even if you could work out the "right" action to take at some point in the future, the situation would have changed in many ways by the time that moment arrived. The only thing we need to concern ourselves with is the present moment.

This has become exceedingly clear to me from the minute I sat down to write this book. To begin with, I almost panicked at how blank my mind was. How would I find enough things to write about for a whole book? But one day as I was walking down the street on an errand, it occurred to me that I didn't have to know the answer to that question then. I couldn't write a whole book immediately. Just like everyone else, I could write only one chapter . . . *No:* one page . . . *No:* one paragraph . . . *No:* one sentence . . . *No:* one word at a time. The thing to do was get started and see what appeared on each page. So this is what I am doing. I have stopped worrying about all the other chapters I may or may not write. I am just typing this sentence, and right here at this moment there is everything I need to be able to complete it.

This is really the way it is with everything else, too.

I had arrived in New York City at the ripe old age of twenty-five with my virginity still intact. I discovered to my dismay that other people found this amusing. "What were you saving it for?" they asked. In England I had defended myself against all comers (pun not intended), certain in the belief that my future husband, whoever he might be, would prefer it that way. Now I wondered how I could divest myself of this embarrassment as quickly as possible. There were certainly plenty of prospects. Young men invited me out all the time, but they seemed to expect that if they paid for the dinner I would sleep with them afterward, and

I never liked any of them enough to reward them in this way.

Eventually a nice young man did turn up. I cannot recall the details of the dinner that must have preceded it. What I remember is that the bed broke under us. It wasn't exactly the way Hemingway described the earth moving under his fictional lovers. The bed, apparently, had a habit of falling apart. For me the experience (of losing my maidenhead) was quite painful and not very enjoyable, but at least and at last the deed was done. Either the young man in question was turned off by my inexperience, or he met someone else the next week. History doesn't relate. But in a curious turn of events, he became my divorce lawyer many years later when I bumped into him and found out that he lived across the street from me. I don't have much faith in lawyers, but I felt that because I had once entrusted him with my body, he was probably safe with my divorce proceedings.

A friend called me the other day. She had been for two job interviews and was worrying about what she should say if one place offered her a job and she hadn't heard from the other but would prefer to work there. This seemed like a nonissue to me. I pointed out that no decision had to be made yet since neither organization had made an offer. When the decision needed to be made she would know exactly what to do, but at the time we were talking any decision would be irrelevant. Many weeks passed, and neither job ever materialized. People waste a lot of time agonizing over something that may never happen.

At one time I was working on a book by Lanza del Vasto, then the leader of the nonviolent movement in France. The translation arrived from him many weeks late, and I had very little time before I had to hand it into production. So I worked all weekend to edit the manuscript. On Monday I wrote to him with various questions. He wrote back very upset. He felt that because I had done all the editing in two days, I could not have been very thorough. "Sometimes," he said, "I agonize all night over just one word." I was nettled. I had had to make up for his tardiness in my spare time, and here he was complaining that I could not have done a proper job so quickly. I responded by saying that I never agonized about just the right word because I didn't believe that agony was helpful. If the right word doesn't come to mind immediately, I simply put a penciled query beside it and come back to it later. By then I will probably be able to come up with what is needed. This method has always worked for me. I don't like agony.

I tend to size up a situation as quickly as possible and then make a move. One of my favorite Michael Crichton dictums from his little-known book, *Travels*, is, "Don't expect other people to read your mind. Read your own mind."

After I had worked at Simon and Schuster for a little while, I asked for an electric typewriter to replace the old manual one I had inherited. Even at a small, impoverished British publishing house like André Deutsch, I had had an electric typewriter. The office manager said that one would be forthcoming, but the months passed and nothing happened. Eventually, I simply went on strike. She marched up to my desk and informed me that I couldn't go on strike because I didn't belong to a union. "But I've already struck," I said. "I have plenty of work to do that isn't typing: filing, reading, etc. When the new typewriter arrives, I'll start to type again."

"But it will take time to get a new typewriter," she responded.

"It's all right," I said. "I'll wait."

An electric typewriter appeared miraculously the next day.

And then there was the time when there was trouble over the dress code. In the mid-sixties people had started wearing miniskirts. This was in the days before panty hose, and my desk was at the end of a very long corridor. The way the desk had been designed left my legs and much else in full view of the world. This was a very unfortunate situation to be in, and I decided to remedy it. I went out and bought a pantsuit. It was a navy blue wool suit with brass buttons, and I wore it with a long-sleeved, high-collared white ruffled shirt. I looked demure but efficient.

Immediately the publisher sent for me. There had been a complaint from the president's office (from his middle-aged narrow-minded female assistant, actually).

"We don't want you to wear that outfit in the office again," he said. "It's not appropriate."

"It's far more appropriate than what all the other women are wearing," I said. "At least I'm not revealing parts of myself that are best kept covered in public."

"If you were working in a bank, you wouldn't be allowed to wear pants," he retorted.

"But I don't work in a bank, Peter. I work in a publishing house. Surely the only person who might have some cause to object is Bob, and he doesn't mind at all."

"You are just being a prima donna," he said. "Are you planning to wear this suit every day?"

"Of course not," I replied. "I never wear the same thing two days running."

"Will you promise me that you won't wear it to the office in the future?"

"I promise you that on the days when I wear this I will not come into the office," I said and turned on my heel and walked out of the room.

Sometimes when you do things quickly, other people get alarmed. After I had been in New York for many years, a handsome young man asked me to marry him. I had had offers before (all in England) but had never felt tempted. It seemed to me that you had to be very certain of something like this before you embarked on it. But this time I was not in any doubt. There was something about Neil Lippe that I recognized. It was as though we had known each other for eternity. It came about like this.

When I first saw Neil I was immediately attracted to him, but something inside me warned me that if I went in that direction, I would get burned, and so I looked away. He told me later that he had looked at me and felt the same strong pull but decided to wait before he did anything about it. He was in his early twenties and not yet ready for any kind of commitment. This was a playboy of the Western world, experimenting with everything that came his way, and I was a rather straitlaced Englishwoman of almost thirty.

Circumstances brought us together again about seven years later, and after just one date, Neil proposed. I was very taken aback and asked if I could have a few days to think about it. But the more I thought about it, the more I realized that there was really no decision to make. The memory of our connection was ancient, and one evening when he was an hour late arriving at my apartment and I began to imagine him under a bus, I accepted, telling him that I had discovered that I couldn't live without him.

Bob Gottlieb did his best to stop me.

"Why are you rushing into this?" he asked. "Maria and I lived together for five years before we got married."

"But that was you and Maria, and this is Neil and me," I responded.

"Marriage is hard," he said. "Take some time to think about this."

"I know that marriage is hard. But life itself is hard. Why not get married and share the difficulties? I know the difference between a wedding and a marriage. I understand that the wedding is just the beginning."

Almost everyone else also did their best to dissuade me. Neil had made no secret of the fact that he had had many gay relationships, but I knew that he had also had two long-term affairs with women and that none of his liaisons with men had lasted as long as his three-year relationships with women. He wanted to put all that behind him and settle down with me. I thought that this took tremendous courage and that with his talents, which were many and varied, and my strength, we could go far together. I had no hesitation in saying yes, and the more people tried to dissuade me, the more we wanted to go ahead.

A few years later Neil came home one evening and said, "In my first year of business I have made three thousand five hundred dollars, so now you can have your baby." (This was in 1977 but, even then, this wasn't a large sum.)

"Three thousand five hundred gross or net?" I asked.

"Gross," he said.

"Well, that's not a great deal, but if everybody waited until they could afford a baby, none would ever be born. Still, it can't be 'my' baby. I need help getting it started, and I'll need even more help once it arrives. Also, if you don't want a baby, we shouldn't even contemplate this. It has to be 'our' baby not 'my' baby."

"I want a baby, too," he said.

And so that night I conceived a child. Again, there were no fireworks or other epiphanies (unfortunately). You may wonder how I can be so sure that the seed was sown that night. What I heard was that this was the moment to get pregnant, so immediately I became open to the opportunity. Also, I had had an infection for the previous ten days, and so there had been no possibility of conception until that moment. Neil said later that he prayed that night that we would have a child who would love God. That may be true, but he didn't mention it at the time.

Exactly two weeks later I started retching. To begin with, I thought it was a recurrence of the hepatitis that I had contracted earlier from Neil. He hadn't realized that he was a carrier or even that he had had hepatitis at all, but it turned out to be in his blood. I was sick from the day of our wedding for many months, and I believed at the time that if our marriage could survive that illness, it could survive anything. On that score I turned out to be wrong.

When the nausea didn't go away, I went to a friend's doctor, and he performed every test under the sun and could find nothing wrong. After two visits and several large bills, I called from my sickbed to say that I still couldn't stop throwing up. I thought that I might be pregnant.

"Why didn't you mention it before?" he asked tartly.

"Doctor," I said, "if an unknown woman comes to you and she hasn't kept any food down for days on end, surely pregnancy is always a possibility? Even if I were not married, there is still such a thing as immaculate conception. It's happened before and it could happen again."

"When did you last see your gynecologist?" he asked.

I told him that it was several weeks earlier but that it had been before I thought I might have conceived.

"How are your breaths?" he asked—or I thought that was what he said. It turned out that he had said "breasts." What on earth did he mean? Apparently, he wanted to know if they were tender or different in any way, but they were not. So he instructed me to come in the next day and bring him a urine sample.

When I arrived in his office, he looked in disdain at what I had brought him and said that there was not enough liquid to test. I told him that he was lucky there was something in the bottle, since I had not managed to keep anything down for days. He gave me an internal exam and said that I had no visible signs of pregnancy. Then he drew some blood and told me to call back a few days later.

When I called, he told me that the result was positive, but he sounded doubtful.

"So I'm pregnant," I announced.

"I'm from Missouri, the 'Show-Me' state," he said. He recommended that I wait a couple of weeks and then go and see my gynecologist again.

"Doctor," I said, "you have known women who have tested negative and then turned out to be pregnant, but not the reverse. The only thing that might cause you to think that I was pregnant is a change in my hormone levels, and you've tested me for that and everything else and you could find nothing."

So I telephoned Neil and said, "Either you have very strong squiggles or you have good aim or both."

"What do you mean?" he asked.

I announced that we were going to have a baby. I think we were both very shocked. It is one thing to decide to get pregnant, and another to have your wish granted a few hours later. I was thirty-eight years old and had never been pregnant before. I had thought that we might have to try for a couple of years before anything happened, and I wouldn't have been surprised if it had turned out to be already too late for me.

In the first couple of months I went from 112 pounds to 100 pounds. I felt queasy for the whole pregnancy, but once my obstetrician threatened to put me on an IV, I stopped vomiting (he said that this threat always worked with his patients). And then I ballooned. By my seventh month I was up to 152 pounds, and all of it was in the front. I lumbered along the street with a watermelon in front of me. I found it impossible to sleep at night because it was then that the baby became active. But it was possible to sleep for an hour at four o'clock in the afternoon. And because I preferred to be horizontal at the moment I fell asleep, I left work each day at 3 so that I would be lying down when 4 P.M. came. Not being able to sleep properly for so many months did teach me one thing: You don't actually have to sleep deeply at night (although it is much nicer if you do), but you do need to rest your body. So if you lie there and rest, a certain amount of refreshment takes place. The main thing is not to fret about the fact that you can't sleep. It is the fretting that makes you feel so terrible. This discovery has stood me in good stead on the very few nights since that time when I have not been able to sleep.

I had no prior experience of taking care of babies, but once Adam arrived, I did not give my inexperience a second thought. I just proceeded from one stage to the next, and somehow the solutions presented themselves naturally. I felt as if I had always known how to hold a baby and care for him. Perhaps I was lucky enough to have an easy child, because I don't remember any disastrous occasions. However, I often found myself puzzled by the attitudes of other parents I met, such as the young couple whose two-year-old insisted on trying to stick his fingers in every electrical socket in our apartment. I kept darting forward to prevent catastrophe, and they just stood by and watched as I told the little boy in no uncertain terms to cease and desist.

"When do you start discipline?" the mother asked. "Is it time to begin?"

"You start from the moment a child is born," I answered. "And you never stop. It is a little late already, but I suggest you start now."

It is usually not a good idea to wait around wondering when to begin something. If an idea comes to you, it is probably because it is the appropriate moment for it. The thought has presented itself because it is needed. See if it can be implemented now rather than letting it molder or fester in the back of your brain. I have found that if I let things languish, they either start to weigh me down or they never come to fruition at all.

SEVEN

The Company We Keep

Human beings are gregarious by nature. We like to spend time alone, but most of us prefer to spend more time with other people than by ourselves. It is our nature to share—a meal, a hug, a conversation, a time and place. I know that just having another person in the room or in the house keeps my consciousness more alert. I can sit quietly all evening with no need to talk or exchange anything out loud, as long as there is someone else there. Now that I am usually alone in the evenings, I find it difficult to maintain the attention necessary to do all I would like to do and often fall asleep over a book or manuscript.

When I was in China, I noticed that I was often unwilling to do certain things unless I had company. By which I mean that I was willing to enter the subway in Shanghai without having any idea how it worked, where it went, and how to pay (and, of course, I do not speak Chinese) simply because I was exploring with another woman. I don't think I would have had the nerve to do this alone. We often draw courage from someone else and can be terrified on our own.

A few years ago I was staying in a wooden cabin in New Mexico, and in the middle of the night I was awoken by the worst thunderstorm I had ever experienced—two whole hours of fork lightning and thunder directly overhead, all reverberating around the wooden walls and visible through all fifteen windows. I was completely terrified. There was nowhere to hide. There was no phone, no lightning conductor, and my hosts in a trailer a few hundred yards away were too far away to hear me scream (so I didn't). I wondered if they would find me in the morning—fried. Of course, I did survive to tell the tale, but I know that my fear would have been less if I had not been alone. What is it that we draw from other people that is so comforting? It is not that we think that they are braver or more capable than we are. Why is there so much strength in numbers?

Not only does the company of others give us the courage to do things we would not do on our own, but we also do all kinds of things for them that we would not be willing (or able) to do for ourselves. I am not just thinking of stories of mothers who have lifted cars off children trapped beneath them.

Recently I joined a small "sitting" group that meets once a week. We sit for three-quarters of an hour. I used to meditate twice a day for half an hour, but for the last few years this has crept back to twenty minutes in the morning and nothing in the evening. Nowadays, after twenty minutes my body has programmed itself to get up from the cushion. So I wasn't sure that I would be able to manage three-quarters of an hour comfortably. I was curious to see what would happen.

The first evening I was fidgety. The following week I settled down immediately, and when the bell sounded at the end of the session, I had a hard time surfacing again. It has continued thus ever since, and I am grateful. Perhaps the reason I am able to sit there longer has to do with not losing face. I don't want to disturb anyone else by getting up after twenty minutes. But I think there are two other factors at work: If someone says "three-quarters of an hour," then I don't question it. The second harks back to what I said earlier about there being strength in numbers. If the other people in the room can do it, well then, so can I. It is a question of meeting the challenge.

One interesting facet of what happens when we are in the company of others is the shifting roles we play. My brother Chris and his middle son recently went on a safari in Africa. The group consisted of six teenage boys, a father, and a guide. Everyone ate and slept outdoors and pitched in with all the chores. I was privileged to read the communal diary that was kept, and the entry that struck me the most was by one of the boys who, after a couple of days of following behind the guide, was asked to be the leader. Instead of relying on a professional to be on the alert and not step on a snake or disturb wild animals, the young man found himself responsible for the safety, indeed the lives, of all his companions. Suddenly all his antennae were out, his senses alert. He went from being rather bored and caught up in his mosquito bites to this new and wondrous state because of his different point of view. He was traveling along the same track in the high grass, but it was now a matter of life and death. He found this enormously empowering. His whole mind and body rose to the challenge. He didn't make a single movement without being aware of what he was doing. He wrote that taking the lead forced him to remain in the present without letting his mind wander off into dreams.

Living alone tends to make you a little selfish. In some ways, you close down rather than open up. Because you do not have to accommodate anyone else, you arrange everything just so (particularly if you happen to be me). This was brought home some years back when I invited someone to live with me. The first evening after he moved in, I returned from the office and he was already sitting in the living room watching television. My hackles rose. For longer than I could remember I had come through the door and decompressed gently. I didn't want to talk to anyone for a little while after I had got off the subway. I just wanted to be quiet, to put my things down, open my mail, make a cup of tea, take my shoes off, and collapse on the sofa. Only then did I feel up to communicating with other people.

That first evening I watched how I felt, and I didn't say anything. After all, I was the one who had invited him into the house. He came, I realized ruefully, with his own habits, and I would need to welcome those too. But the second night it upset me even more, and so I told him how I felt and asked him if I could have just five minutes' quiet. This was all I needed. After that, he was nice enough to turn the television off as soon as he heard my key in the door and ask me later if it was okay to turn it back on. It is always the little things that get on our nerves.

As I said earlier, Neil and I went out on only one date before he asked me to marry him ten days later. I suspect that it was something he said that first evening that convinced me to say yes. We were eating dinner at his favorite French restaurant, and I was regaling him with my customary patter. For some time he watched me without saying anything. Indeed, I don't think he was really listening. He was just observing me. And then he leaned forward and said, "Why do you always hold yourself back?"

I stopped in my tracks. No one had ever noticed this before. Indeed, I had never even acknowledged to myself that I used my ability to tell stories as a kind of articulate armor that would protect me from all slings and arrows. I didn't know how to respond, but I was grateful that someone had at last spotted this. I felt both uncovered and discovered—disarmed but acknowledged. This was a level of honesty I had rarely encountered. I suspect that I hoped that this would be just the first of many revelations. Here was a man who would act as my mirror, reflecting back to me the things about myself that I needed to know.

Unfortunately, this was the only occasion on which he did this. Still, it provided enough of a shock to show me that my defenses needed to come down fast if I wanted a true meeting with another human being. I became aware that it is not possible to meet anyone if you are not available. Many of us try to protect ourselves in this way, but we need to remember that walls keep out not only our enemies but also our friends. Since that time I have done my best to be available to anyone or anything that needs me. I don't always manage it, but I try.

This word *available* is an interesting word. It turns out that *avail*, meaning "to be of use, assist, or help" comes from the Latin *valere*, "to be strong, to be worthy." This is remarkable, in that when I was younger, I wanted to be useful, and now I try to be available. I had thought that they were two different concepts but now that I have consulted a dictionary, I see how they are related. Also, I understand why being available to others carries with it such a sense of strength and value. It is right there in the root of the word.

When I began working at Knopf, it was as Bob Gottlieb's assistant, but gradually I took on other roles as well. For one thing, I started to sell reprint rights, which are the licensing rights to reproduce a company's books in paperback and other formats. It was a given at Knopf in the early 1970s that anyone could edit books, provided they didn't stint on the job for which they were being paid. So, although I had no degree, I soon found myself acquiring books that interested me, particularly books of spiritual teaching. As my small list of books and authors grew, I saw them as providing "good company" for the people who read them. Plotinus expressed it well:

For the absolute good is the cause and source of all beauty, just as the sun is the source of all daylight, and it cannot therefore be spoken or written; yet we speak and write of it, in order to start and escort ourselves on the way, and arouse our minds to the vision: like as when one showeth a pilgrim on his way to some shrine that he would visit: for the teaching is only of whither and how to go, the vision itself is the work of him who hath willed to see.

After I had edited fifty books, I asked if I could start an imprint at Random House devoted exclusively to spiritual books, books that nourish the soul, illuminate the mind, and speak directly to the heart, and in 1989 I was given the go-ahead to create an imprint as part of Harmony which already published books of a similar nature. When the question of a name came up, I suggested "In Good Company," my idea being that each title would be "A Good Companion" that would "escort pilgrims on the way." The powers-that-be vetoed this idea, declaring that it sounded like a bevy of old ladies in a retirement home, so reluctantly I chose another name: Bell Tower.

I worked for some months to distill the essence of what I had learned in my life so far, teachings I wanted to share with the world at large. When Bell Tower's first three books were published in the spring of 1991, this message appeared in calligraphy on a small bookmark in each copy:

> *The pure sound of the bell summons us into the present moment.*
> *The timeless ring of truth is expressed in many different voices,*
> *each one magnifying and illuminating the sacred.*
> *The clarity of its song resonates within us*
> *and calls us away from those things which often distract us*
> *—that which was, that which might be—*
> *to That Which Is.*

At the end of 1996 I was on a retreat with meditation teacher Toni Packer at the Santa Sabina Center in San Rafael, California. One day, as I was silently pacing around the cloister, I spotted something familiar on one of the tables. There was a big poster of Thomas Merton and before it a candle and a tall, thin piece of calligraphy. When I stopped to read it, my heart stopped too. It was a blow-up of the bookmark. Later (when we were allowed to speak again), I discovered that the nuns liked the statement so much they used it at the beginning of many of their workshops. Finding what I had written five years earlier on display three thousand miles away was a very heartwarming experience. It showed me that there was indeed a universal *sangha,* a company of men and women on the path of truth who appreciated the signposts I had erected.

I spoke earlier about not taking what is not yours unless it is freely offered. The other side of the coin is making sure to share with others what you believe *is* yours. By which I mean everything that is currently in your possession. I mentioned earlier that all the stuff that we are currently responsible for—goods, money, a house, a car—is just ours for the time being. Like us, it is just passing through creation. Sometimes when I spend more money on something than I feel comfortable with, I tell myself that I am helping the economy. What goes around comes around. If you continually offer to others what you have right now, the chances are that whatever you need later will find its way to you from one source or another. I visited Russia not long after the breakup of the Soviet Union. None of the people I met seemed to have a ruble to their name but I discovered that whenever a friend, neighbor, or relative needed money for an emergency, everyone pitched in. Wherever this loan money came from (and I never found out the answer to that question), it seemed to circulate in the atmosphere, always becoming available to whoever needed it. If we don't put a strong claim on our possessions, then we don't feel a lack when we pass them on to others.

Although I enjoy being alone for periods of time, I am happiest in the company of others. This is because in another person it is always possible to see our own reflection, to see who we really are. You need to be still for this to happen, or there is a distortion in the mirror. You also need to be quiet. It doesn't happen often, but when it does . . . Perhaps this is why we are all so drawn to babies. We want to gaze directly into their eyes. We want to see and be seen. The same thing happens when we are in love. In ordinary life so much time is spent in talking, in avoiding other people's eyes. But when (at last) you are comfortable with someone else alone and in silence, just looking, there is a true meeting, and words drop away. They no longer have a place. They are a distraction, a limitation, a hindrance to the blazing fullness of it all.

EIGHT

Giving Attention

Years later, when my ex-husband, Neil, was dying, I remember asking Ram Dass what I could do for him. Somehow, until that moment, my loved ones had always died offstage, and I had no experience in such a situation. He told me just to give Neil my full attention, if possible coordinating my breathing with his. Giving others our complete attention is such a simple thing, and yet we rarely remember to do it. Whether the person we are with is dying or living, this is always one of the greatest treasures we can give them. When I thought about it, I realized that when I myself was in the hospital with hepatitis, my friend Katharine just came and sat there, waiting on me, as it were. Everyone else seemed under the impression that they had to entertain or engage me in some way. It was such a relief when she came. After each visit I felt as though she had actually brought me energy while the others had drained it away.

From time to time I will be in the middle of a conversation with a friend and am suddenly aware that he is no longer listening. If that happens, I stop speaking and wait a minute. The silence is often enough to bring him back. Perhaps he was off on his own train of thought, but wherever he was, he was no longer hearing me. Of course, I have often been guilty of this myself, although no one I know has tried the same trick on me. I generally return from my "vacation" and desperately try to figure out what my companion has just said.

Not only do most of us not listen very carefully to what other people are saying, we also rarely listen to ourselves. And if we are not willing to listen to our own voices, then why should anyone else bother? You will find that if you start listening to what you say as you say it (and I am not talking about rehearsing it in your head beforehand), you will discover that you speak with more clarity and it is much easier for the other person to hear you. There is a great power in attention.

Attention is at its most miraculous when you start to use it. To begin with, it is only when you bring all your senses to bear on whatever you plan to do next that you will know how to proceed. We tend to approach most things with preconceived ideas. We carry forward whatever we noticed on earlier occasions in the belief that it will be very useful this time. In fact, there is an unspoken assumption that we do not really need to pay that much attention this time because "we've done it before." But no two situations are exactly the same, and such a habit can be very costly. Centuries ago Heraclitus pointed out that you cannot step twice into the same river, and hardly any of us have taken his observation to heart.

I am not a very technical person, but I have discovered that I can solve many household problems just by bringing myself into the present, contemplating what is in front of me, and waiting for inspiration to arrive. One day I came home from the office and went to the closet to get something. When I glanced down, I saw a note and a few screws on the floor right next to the polisher. It was from my Brazilian cleaning lady, and it read: "This machine it dusnt work." I hauled the polisher out and sat down on the floor beside it. I started to take it apart, one piece at a time, hoping to catch sight of where the missing pieces might fit. And, indeed, about twenty minutes later I had reassembled everything and got it to work (don't ask me how).

The main thing to remember when you are faced with a physical task is that you need to put your full attention at the place where the work is being done. For instance, if you are hammering a nail into the wall, you may think that the place to focus on is the head of the nail. However, the work is actually taking place where the nail is going into the wall, so put your mind at that precise point while your eyes watch the hammer hit the nail. This will enable the nail to go straight into the wall. If you are trying to unscrew a recalcitrant jar lid, let your attention rest in that space between the metal and the glass as you twist. You may think that there isn't any space there, but obviously there must be or the two would be welded together. I once applied this principle to pulling poison ivy roots out of the undergrowth. I let my mind travel the length of the root, allowing it to come to rest at the point where the root went into the ground, and I left my attention there in that space between the root and the earth as I gently pulled the plant toward me. And the long, white root came out of the earth without any argument.

The other place where there is a space and yet we overlook it is between ourselves and the situation. The Tibetan Buddhist teacher Chögyam Trungpa said, "Once one is aware of the space between the situation and oneself, then anything can happen in that space. Whatever occurs does so in the midst of space. Nothing takes place 'here' or 'there' in terms of relationship or battle."

Over the years I have noticed a remarkable thing, and that is that I can trust each situation. What I am talking about is that I like to get things taken care of the moment I spot them, if not before. If there is dust on the sideboard, I want to clean it now and not wait until Sunday morning, which is when I would normally do it. However, from time to time something needs to be done (such as calling the painter to come in and repaint my son's room now that he has left home. This is something I have been meaning to do since he left eight days ago), and I just don't do it. When I first observed this seeming reluctance, I decided that it was sloth, but gradually I came to the conclusion that it was because it was simply not the right moment. If I am not taking care of something that is obvious, it is because I need to wait for the universe to get into the right mode. You certainly need to discriminate about this because for some people it may indeed be laziness. However, knowing myself the way I do, I find it amusing to watch how the days go by and I am still not moved to take action. So I just let whatever it is sit quietly in my mind for the time being. Then, suddenly, I make my move. I guess this is rather like a lizard catching its lunch. (Sorry: this is not the happiest of metaphors, but it is what sprang into my mind. I see this lizard immobile on a rock, and then its tongue streaks out and catches a fly or whatever.)

It is the same when you cannot remember someone's name. It is no good searching for it desperately. If I do this I usually draw a blank. However, if I let everything go, a few minutes later the name will drift into my mind without more ado (well, more often than not). Things happen when they happen, in their own good time.

It is the nature of thoughts to circulate. If they have floated into your mind once, they will undoubtedly float in again, so there is no need to grasp them. I find that they operate rather like a lazy Susan. When I sit down to meditate (or lie in the bath. I have trained myself to stay in the bath for a little while after I am clean—just lying there in the water with my mind at rest. I have discovered that all kinds of things come into my mind that I am normally too busy to entertain), there is a great temptation to open my eyes and make a note of something that I need to do once I get up from my cushion. But I have learned that this isn't really necessary. Whatever it was that came up surfaced because I was no longer suppressing it or overwhelming it with a host of other urgent things. If I just allow it to be there along with all the other things that arise, it will still be there later. The same thing happens as I go to sleep. Whatever drifts in as I am about to go to sleep, will be right there first thing in the morning. There is no need to turn the light on and search for a pencil and pad and make your mind active again. A little trust is called for.

In 1972 I edited a translation of the *Tao Te Ching* by Gia-fu Feng and Jane English. Eventually the time came when I had to write jacket copy for the book. This is the moment that every editor dreads because you have to find a way to express the essence of the book in a few sentences so that a reader will grasp immediately what the book has to offer. I was daunted at the prospect of reducing this sixth-century-B.C. classic to a single paragraph. Weeks went by, and finally I had only twenty minutes left. I sat down before the typewriter, and my mind went blank (not deliberately). I waited a little while and then began to type. What appeared on the page arrived whole. Now, thirty years later, I would not alter a word of the copy on the outside of the book:

> Accept what is in front of you without wanting the situation to be other than it is. Study the natural order of things and work with it rather than against it, for to try to change what *is* only sets up resistance. Nature provides everything without requiring payment or thanks, and also provides for all without discrimination—therefore let us present the same face to everyone and treat all people as equals, however they may behave. . . . We serve whatever or whoever stands before us, without any thought for ourselves. *Te*—which may be translated as "virtue" or "strength"—lies always in *Tao*, or "natural law." In other words: Simply be.

After this I realized, somewhat ruefully, that it was not writing the copy that took time but the not-writing of it. The not-writing was a tremendous burden that I had carried around unnecessarily for weeks.

I have never quite understood what people mean when they say that making decisions is hard. My experience is that if I have to do something, I look at it as clearly as possible and just move forward. There seems to be only one possibility, and I pursue it. If I really don't know what to do, then I do nothing. Eventually, as I said above, the universe shifts, and whatever needs doing becomes obvious. Until it is the right moment, there *is* nothing that can be done.

Think of all those days when you have gone shopping for a particular item and you are thwarted at every turn. We all have those days when nothing seems to go right, and the hard part is accepting that this is not one of those times when your plans are going to come to fruition. Yesterday, for instance, the painter was going to come to give me an estimate for painting the room, but he canceled. This left the whole day free for writing and other things, but everything I had wanted to do didn't get done. My sister-in-law, Valery, had written me a long e-mail regarding a paper she had just given at a conference in Florence on the Neoplatonist Marsilio Ficino and his views on philosophy and politics. The paper contained the word *myrobalan*. I was mystified, and then I remembered that I had the *Oxford English Dictionary* on CD-ROM and here was the perfect moment to refer to it. I had used it only a handful of times since I had received it as a present a couple of months back. That's when the first disaster struck: The computer refused to read the data disc, and even though I uninstalled the program and reinstalled it, the whole thing kept freezing. I consulted the booklet and saw to my horror that the warranty lasted only sixty days and had therefore expired the day before. I kept hoping that a miracle would occur. I dusted the CD-ROM. I treated it gently. But however often I loaded it in, no miracle happened. I won't bore you with all the other small things that went awry (but I will tell you that a *myrobalan* is a very bitter medieval plum). I just wanted to give you the flavor of how a myriad of details can appear to thwart the progress of a happy day. Of course, I did get some things done but not the ones that satisfied my heart. And therein lies the secret.

We are so set on accomplishing the things we want to do—fulfilling our desires—that we don't want to see what needs to be done right in front of us.

Yes, I walked to the farmers' market (twenty blocks there and twenty blocks back; got my body energized). And I bought long, slim, mauve eggplants, crisp green beans, a bunch of young leeks, small sweet potatoes, and shining vermilion and yellow peppers, and then made three pans of roasted vegetables drizzled with oil and sprinkled with herbs, so that I have the makings of meals for myself for several days. I also cleaned some silver, re-covered a disintegrating cushion, and so on, but I saw all those things as hindrances to what I really wanted to do. Yet all the chores I took care of were necessary, and it would have been much more enjoyable if I hadn't had this internal argument going on about the fact that I should have been writing, that I was "wasting" time. What we are doing right now is what we are doing right now. Wanting a different scenario is useless. This is the movie we have rented, so why not watch it? The other movies aren't available or haven't been released yet.

One of the most practical teachings I have received in my life is "Go through the door that's open." We get all kinds of ideas in our heads as to what we think we would like to do, and most of them bear no relation to what is likely or possible. This is not like trying to unlock a door to which you have no key; it is more like trying to walk through a wall. Have a clear look at what is in front of you, and you will recognize the way to go. But it does have to be a very clear look.

I have only just seen that this is the answer to one of my besetting sins. Those that know me well are aware that I have an annoying habit: I complain a lot—even though, as someone pointed out to me last year, there is really no point in complaining unless it is to someone who can remedy the situation. But (at least in my case) reason doesn't always kick in when things seem unfair: I start to whine more often than not. This is something I know I need to work on, and I apologize now to all those friends to whom I should have apologized long ago. When we (read "I") complain, it is because we believe that things should be other than they are. Who was it who said, "The rain falls equally on the just and upon the unjust, but the unjust has the just's umbrella"? Why didn't I take to heart the first sentence of that *Tao Te Ching* copy I wrote so long ago?

If the computer has a conniption and you are put

on hold by the techies for twenty minutes, that's the way it is. Complaining about it upsets you, and it also upsets those who have to listen to your complaints, so what have you achieved? It does not solve anything. In the end it all boils down to our attitude. If you eat nothing for two weeks, you could call it a fast or you could see it as starvation. If you are confined to one room for several years, you could view it as a punishment or as an opportunity. One of my favorite authors, Charles Morgan, was taken prisoner as a British naval officer during World War I and held captive in Holland for four years. He used the time away from the responsibility of earning a living to write a novel. He considered this period in his life a blessing and went on to write many more novels and win several prestigious literary prizes. Next time I am on hold, I need to remember this and put the time to good use.

I have a friend who lives in Arizona who tells me he likes to come to New York City, where he is constantly caught up in traffic. It gives him the chance to sit and meditate for a little while. This isn't possible where he lives because in the desert there are long stretches of road with no traffic lights and no chance to do anything but keep driving. He is the only person I know who seems to enjoy stopping at the lights.

A key issue we often overlook is our own attitude. Someone once said to me: "Everything is fine as it is. Your view of it may or may not be." In his book *Travels,* Michael Crichton pointed out that the most valuable thing we can possess is a perspective, a new way of looking at things. "The purpose of education is to provide perspectives. . . . Any new perspective alters consciousness."

What I have discovered is that not only does a different view of things change the outcome but so does a different form. When I make bread, I always use the same recipe (whole-wheat flour, dry yeast, salt, water), but I don't necessarily make a round loaf each time. Sometimes I make a long loaf, and sometimes I make rolls. When I take the bread out of the oven, the texture and the taste are different, depending on the shape and size. This never fails to surprise me. Early in the 1970s I shared a brownstone with some friends. Since we all enjoyed fresh bread, we would take turns doing the baking each day, and we signed up for however much we needed: half a loaf, two loaves, whatever. We were all using the same ingredients and the same recipe, but the bread always turned out differently, depending on who made it. In fact, you could tell who had baked bread that day by looking at it and picking it up. The taste and appearance of the bread usually reflected the character of the baker. Some people baked high, fluffy loaves with lots of holes in them but little taste. Others produced indigestible, stonelike offerings. What did I bake? Very compact, tasty loaves, of course. I could never make my loaves rise the way I wanted them to, but they always tasted delicious.

I encountered a couple of tai chi chuan teachers recently who focus on this principle. They have understood that if you free the body from mechanical movements, you also free the mind from mechanical thoughts. As one put it, "The moment you change your physical position, it changes the way you think."

The opposite is also true: If you change the flow of energy, you change the structure. When a moment of clarity comes, we move naturally from a contorted position and vice versa. Straighten your back and become balanced, and your head will also clear.

A year or so after Neil left, I was at a party and someone came over and asked about my husband and new baby. I told him that my baby was fine but that my husband had left when Adam was a year and a quarter. He looked at me for a moment and then said, "So you must be almost over it by now?" The question hung in the air as he held my gaze. This was not the usual cocktail chitchat. I took a deep breath and replied, "I don't think you ever get over it, but perhaps with time things recede into perspective." And then I burst into tears. Perspective is indeed all-important.

I was just on the phone with my friend David, describing how events in my life seem to arise and make their way into this book within a few days. It is not exactly recycling; it is more like cycling. "Re" makes it sound as though something is being repeated, but that is not the way it feels. He suggested that I am calling these situations out of the universe (I am not sure how he expressed it, but that was what I heard). Come to think of it, one of my criteria for selecting a book for publication is whether what the author has written in the manuscript changes my own spiritual practice. If it can do that for me, I believe it can do the same for others. So much of the teaching I receive these days comes from the manuscripts that people send to me. I know that these writers think that they are looking for a publisher, but perhaps their manuscripts keep arriving here because they contain whatever it is I need to learn next. What a revolutionary idea! And yet the sages have always known this. "When the student is ready, the teacher will appear" (and vice versa). The teacher doesn't have to be a flesh-and-blood person. Anything or anyone can be a teacher. In fact, whatever is right in front of you is your teacher.

The idea that whatever is in front of you has something to teach you is extraordinary. A few years back, Adam, who knows more about movies than I ever will, mentioned that he was going to see *Pocahontas*. I thought it strange that a college kid would go to see a Disney movie, but he doesn't do things lightly, and so I inquired why he was going. I should mention that he was majoring in film and video. "I can always learn something from a movie," he said, "even if it's how not to make one." It *is* sometimes hard to glean a scrap of wisdom from a trip to the supermarket or wherever, but it is there if you can spot it.

Whatever it is, you can learn from it. No need to waste any experience, even (particularly) the telephone conversation I just had with David. There I was bemoaning to him (I had already bemoaned to myself) that the morning had disappeared and I still hadn't got down to any writing. I felt guilty. This happens day after day. I think it is because almost everyone has been telling me that good writing happens in the morning. Armed with that idea, I have been failing morning after morning for the last month or so. But the thing is: I find that the writing does happen spontaneously (providing I start typing. Without that, it certainly doesn't happen at all), which is the way I had hoped it would when I decided to write this book. Earlier today, I didn't have this material to write about. Now that David has called, I do. So we are back to just accepting things as they are and not wanting them to be some other way—or perhaps this is another way of seeing how we have no alternative but to go through the door that is open.

Sometimes I am not at all sure what circumstances are teaching me. As I said, I prefer to do everything immediately, just as soon as I think about it. This can be awkward because thoughts can distract you at any moment of the day. In an ideal world you keep your mind on what you are doing, and no stray thought would dare enter your mind, but the ideal often seems very unattainable. If you drop everything the moment a new thought occurs to you, you will just leave a trail of unfinished jobs behind you. The best solution I have come up with is to make a note of whatever it is and go firmly back to what I was doing before. That way, at least I haven't completely lost track of it for the day. The thought will, of course, return at some later moment, but if you want to take care of whatever it was next, it is safer to make a note now (unless you are meditating or about to go to sleep). The main thing is not to panic when all kinds of new ideas come flooding into your head one after the other. Think of them as a plus rather than a minus: The juices are flowing. Hurrah! Oh, and make sure that when you make your note, it is legible. Far too often I have made a note to myself that I have not been able to read later. This is because I have very bad handwriting. I am ashamed of how bad it is. I think of myself as a very orderly person, and yet why is it that after all these years my handwriting is still so terrible?

One of the lessons I learned quite early in my life is that whatever you seem worst at is perhaps where an undiscovered talent lies. It is as though we deliberately ignore our own talents and go out of our way to deny them. I discovered this when I was attending classes at the philosophy school and I was the one chosen to go back to the London school for a week, learn the rudiments of a particular calligraphy discipline, and return to New York to teach it to the other students. At first I thought the person who had asked me to do this was out of her mind. I pointed out that I had the most dreadful handwriting in the whole group. But apparently that was one of the reasons I had been chosen. And so I flew to London, devoted an entire week to calligraphy, and went on to be in charge of calligraphy in New York for many years, delighting in the forms of the letters and the spaces they described. (It did wonders for my calligraphy but unfortunately nothing for my handwriting.) I observed the same principle in action with another student who was very feisty and always causing problems. Eventually this man was asked to teach the class on a day when the tutor was absent, and he took it over as if to the manner born. He never caused trouble in the class after that.

In order to see what is going on at any given moment, we need to have our attention directed out rather than in. Instead of being carried along by the flow of events or withdrawing from it, we just stay right here. There is only *this* moment. This is the only method of appreciating the divine.

We are always anticipating that something better (or worse) is about to happen, but we would do well to keep in mind that wonderful Gahan Wilson cartoon in which two men are sitting on cushions in the zendo and have obviously been there for some time. The monk leans over and whispers into the ear of the novice: "Nothing happens next. This is it."

I don't quite know how we got it into our heads that whatever is happening right now is probably not that important and can be dispensed with, but it is a very pervasive view even though in 1242 Zen Master Dogen observed:

Each day is valuable. . . . Do not compare it with a dragon's bright pearl. A dragon's pearl may be found. But this one day out of a hundred years cannot be retrieved once it is lost.

I just paused before I typed the last sentence. I was mulling over what Dogen had said and marveling that more than seven centuries had elapsed and that most people have still not grasped its significance. As I sat here, I suddenly heard the sparrows chirping outside my window, the trundling of the road-working equipment, the tires swishing on the wet street, as well as the underlying hum of electricity in my office. Up until that moment I had been deaf to all this, having narrowed my attention to the screen in front of me. What is even stranger is that as I started to acknowledge all these sounds, I realized that I had lost track of how my body felt or whether I could smell or taste anything. We have five senses, and we tend to use only one at a time. Such a wealth of impressions is available to us at any given moment, and yet we crowd it out by paying attention only to whatever is going on in our heads.

Our attention is either in or out. This is very clear in meditation but not always apparent at other times. If we are focusing on some idea or problem, we miss everything going on outside. If we welcome impressions from the outside, then we do not get seduced by our own thoughts. It is obvious when you think about it: You can't be in two places at once. So, stay here. Don't go away.

All of us can rise to an emergency. When such a thing happens, it does not occur to us to opt out. We just move forward to do whatever needs to be done, drawing on reserves of knowledge and strength we didn't know we possessed. There is undoubtedly more than one factor involved. An emergency calls us into the present, and immediately the adrenaline necessary to the task floods our system. It is in many ways an impersonal thing; it has to do with the way nature preserves the species. What I find interesting about these situations is that once you are "there," completely present, you feel as though you could do anything. This can happen even in very small ways. For instance, from time to time I have been standing at the kitchen sink, wiping glasses with a dish towel, and suddenly a glass has slipped from my grasp. I have very quick reflexes, and almost without exception I will catch the glass before it smashes to the ground. I may have been in a dream when the glass escaped, but immediately there is a need all my senses are working and I am ready to tackle anything. Most of the time we are off somewhere in our heads and don't experience this sense of urgency, which is why accidents happen in the first place.

NINE

Offer No Resistance

When I lived in England, I often answered "No" to people and events, or, at least, that is how I remember it. Once I had said "Yes" to Bob Gottlieb and his offer of a job in New York—which I did almost on a whim—I continued to respond that way, and it was a profound transformation. I'm not sure how this happened, but I am glad that it did.

Saying no takes so much more effort than saying yes. This doesn't mean that you meekly accept other people's outrageous behavior. What I am talking about is looking at what is before you and welcoming it if it seems appropriate. An opportunity that is presented to you is a present (a gift) and it calls you into the present (now). What most of us tend to do with the maelstrom of opportunities that besiege us is ignore them. Ignoring implies that you know something is there but you choose not to pay attention to it. This can take up a lot of psychic energy. It is a very deliberate act. I usually accept what comes along unless there is a very good reason not to. For instance, if someone calls to invite me to dinner or an event when I have nothing planned for that particular time and it is not something I am sure I would hate, I am reluctant to say no because refusing is like turning my back on what the world is offering. You just never know what each invitation or opportunity holds or where it might lead.

I was discussing this point with my friend Deb one day while circling the reservoir in Central Park, and she disputed my reasoning. A mutual friend had given her my name and number and encouraged her to call me at least a year or so before we met, but she kept not doing anything about it. Eventually we encountered each other through a different connection, and she was quite taken aback that I had materialized in her life anyway. She told me that it had been easier not to call me than to call me, but I don't agree with her. Not doing something may *feel* easier, but it really isn't. All those months when she didn't call me I was hovering in her unconscious and taking up unnecessary room.

After I had been working at Simon and Schuster for more than three years, Bob was hired to run Alfred A. Knopf, and he said that I was welcome to go with him if I wanted to but that I should think carefully before making a decision. There might be many jobs opening up at S&S (two other senior executives were moving to Knopf in addition to Bob). It would not have occurred to me to leave Bob because I had become very attached to him, so I accompanied him to Knopf. Nineteen years later, when he came to tell me that he was quitting Knopf for *The New Yorker*, he didn't ask me to go with him, and so it didn't occur to me to raise the possibility.

I also embraced the situation as it presented itself when I was in my early thirties and a number of students at the philosophy school were looking for apartments and someone suggested that instead of us all paying rent, we should buy a house. I had never owned property. Once the idea arose, however, it seemed the obvious thing to do. There were ten of us needing somewhere to live and five who could put up money for a down payment. A brownstone on the Upper West Side of Manhattan materialized almost immediately, and the only problem seemed to be that no bank was willing to give a mortgage to five professional men and women who had no debts and no financial responsibilities. This was my first experience of the peculiar way the American economy works. It transpired that a bank would lend you money only if you already had debt and had therefore established yourself as creditworthy. Never mind that if you had incurred one debt and had not finished paying it off you were probably not in a position to take on another one. The banks told us that if we formed a corporation, they would give us a mortgage, but we didn't want to do that because then we would have been unable to claim individual tax deductions. Luckily the building's owner was willing to give us a purchase money mortgage at an extraordinarily reasonable rate, and so the deed was done.

We were the happy owners of a five-story brownstone that had been turned into ten apartments, although much of renovation still remained to be done. So the next thing we did was start renovating. I learned a great deal about sanding, painting, electricity, and plumbing—all on-the-job training. Our spare time was given over to working on the house, and when I left to get married four years later, the renovation was still in progress.

Those of us who lived in the building all had different responsibilities. One person was in charge of the finances, another the boiler, a third the garbage, a fourth the garden, and so on. My responsibility was to care for everyone who lived in the house in a general way—someone had to be nominally in charge—and to keep the peace. This led to some interesting situations, including the following one.

Two of the people who moved in were a high-school teacher and her sixteen-year-old ward, Lorraine. As it turned out, there was some friction between them, and shortly after their arrival the guardianship came up for renewal, and it was decided not to continue it. I offered to become responsible for Lorraine, and we went to family court to make this official. This was a very long-drawn-out procedure requiring several appearances and much investigation. Lorraine had been assigned a guardian by the Bureau of Child Welfare when her mother had taken her to court three years earlier on a PINS petition (Person in Need of Supervision). The bureau suspected that we were running a

commune and tried to block the transfer of guardianship. I pointed out to our legal aid lawyer that if it
were a commune, we would be sharing expenses,
which we were not—unfortunately for me. Then they
said that the building was unsuitable because there
were single men living in it. I countered by saying that
each of the two single men occupied his own apartment on the garden floor while Lorraine was living
on the fifth floor but that also, if there were an apartment building in the city in which young men did not
live, there was probably something peculiar about it.
In the end we got the bureau disallowed in the courtroom because of its prejudice. When I eventually came
before the black woman judge, she asked me only one
question: "What do you see as your responsibility toward this child?"

I took a deep breath and replied, "To know where she
is at all times—physically, emotionally, spiritually . . ."
I was about to continue, but the judge cut in:

"Precisely. The child is placed on probation, and
the condition of the probation is that she live with
Miss Rees. Case dismissed."

The proceedings were over almost before they had
begun. We all filed out, and I asked the psychiatric

social worker what the ruling meant. She explained that because the Bureau of Child Welfare had not been allowed in the courtroom, Lorraine had been reassigned from the bureau to the Probation Office. Unfortunately, the Probation Office had no funds and so, although we had achieved our aim, there was not going to be money from any of the agencies to support Lorraine. She offered to take me to the Welfare Department and work with me to obtain some funding. She was as good as her word. She went with me over and over again, but I had to wait until a new mayor was elected before I got any money. I was grateful to John Lindsay when he overhauled the system and we began to get an allowance and food stamps. In the interim, various friends helped us out.

My mother was dismayed when she heard about Lorraine. I pointed out that she had been after me for years about a grandchild. Now I had provided her with one, and she shouldn't complain. Apparently she had not expected a sixteen-year-old grandchild. She had been thinking of a husband (first) and then a baby. She asked me why I had done this, and I explained that I could tell her *how* I had done it but not *why*. Lorraine had needed a home, and I happened to be available. I quoted her the words of Sir George Mallory when he was asked why he had climbed Everest: "Because it was there."

Lorraine was in my care for three years. They were very thorny years because she was a tomboy and a real handful, but it never occurred to me not to do my best for her. I had made a commitment to the judge and to Lorraine, and I wasn't about to reneg on either commitment.

Eventually, things got really out of control. Lorraine would disappear overnight, and I wouldn't know where she was. I told her that if she was not going to use her room, we would offer it to someone else. Space is always at a premium in New York City. I said that the next time she stayed out all night without permission she could look for somewhere else to live. A short time later she vanished for a whole weekend. I called the kind psychiatric social worker to find out what the legal situation was and discovered that if no term is set for probation, then it is just for one year. No one had bothered to let me know this. Apparently, after the first year the responsibility should have been her parents'. So Lorraine left our house on West Ninety-fifth Street and set off for "fresh woods and pastures new." A couple of times she has been back to visit, and she still calls me from California every few years to chat and to ask my advice but not take it.

If I had said no to taking on Lorraine in the beginning, I would have missed out on so much. I really had no experience with young people, and everything I learned during our time together stood me in good stead when my own offspring finally arrived. Even if you start out with little or no affection for someone, once you care for her over a long period, this "caring for" turns into "caring about," and then into love. People often asked me whether I would have picked her to be my child if I had had a choice. We were so different from each other. It always seemed a ridiculous question to me. Even if your child emerges from your own body, you don't get a choice about the kind of person he or she is. Babies just arrive, willy-nilly, and you start loving them right away.

The other trick we often try (on ourselves) in order to avoid dealing with what is in front of us is changing the circumstances. This usually does not solve anything. It just postpones the moment when we have to face whatever it is. Some people are always changing jobs, and others go from one "life" partner to another. For instance, the few men I have fallen in love with have always been unavailable. Often they live thousands of miles away. Sometimes they are married to other people, and the man I did marry was gay. Perhaps if these men had been available, I would have overlooked them. One day I need to see who is right in front of me instead of looking somewhere else and repeating the same mistake over and over.

Both Neil and I tried to make our marriage work (I think), but one evening when Adam was a year and a quarter, Neil said that he needed three months by himself. He didn't know whether he would return. I was shocked and bewildered. In many respects I am very old-fashioned. If I make a vow, I keep it, no matter what the cost. *Divorce* was not in my vocabulary. However difficult the marriage had been, it would never have occurred to me to leave it. I asked him why he was doing this.

"Our marriage has problems," he said.

"Every marriage has problems," I replied. "But once you identify what they are, you try to fix them. You don't just walk out."

I offered to go with him to a marriage counselor if he thought that would help, even though I myself had never contemplated any kind of therapy. But he said that he had all the tools he needed from the philosophy school (where we had met and which we were both still attending). I pointed out that having the tools and using them were two different things, but the next morning he left and, in fact, never returned.

When three months had passed, I asked Neil if there was any chance of his coming back to live with us. I told him that I was considering renting out half of the apartment, both to bring in extra income and also to help one night a week with the baby-sitting. I didn't want to embark on this if there was a possibility he might return. But he said that there was not, and so I moved my bed into a corner of the living room and offered the spare bedroom and bathroom to the universe, wondering who would come and occupy it.

I never advertised, but for some years there was a steady stream of people who came and went—a young Swiss woman who enjoyed mountaineering and liked to walk up and down the six flights of stairs to keep herself in shape, an Episcopalian priest who worked in the city during the week and went back to his home on weekends, an organist and choirmaster who eventually departed without paying the last month's rent, someone who wanted to take a sabbatical from her marriage, a couple from New Jersey who needed a pied-à-terre, and several others. I rented the space furnished and asked each tenant to pay half the rent and baby-sit one evening a week. The latter was always a problem. Even though there were seven nights in each week, no one wanted to make such a commitment. Some offered alternatives: a week's groceries from the supermarket her husband owned (since I never knew when this would kick in, it was possible to ask only for paper goods and Kitty Litter, things that didn't spoil), a massage (this from the woman taking a sabbatical from her marriage, and who was training to be a masseuse. This would have been a great trade but didn't often happen because she came home from school so late, and I didn't like to remind her of our bargain), and so on.

I really enjoyed the company, and it brought me into contact with people I might never have met, but eventually I began to feel as though I was living in Grand Central Terminal. This being New York, almost no one stayed more than six months. After that, a major shift would occur in their lives and they would move on. So at a certain point I went to Bob Gottlieb and said that I didn't want to do this anymore. I wanted my home to myself. He said that he thought this was a great idea, but I pointed out that unless he was willing to give me a raise equal to the amount I would be losing, I couldn't do it. He gave it to me without hesitation, and I was torn between gratitude and relief—and anger that he had not offered this chunk of money years earlier.

This year when I went home to take care of my mother, I fought a silent battle with her every evening. Books no longer hold her attention, and she likes to watch television. She turns the volume up very loud because she doesn't like to wear her hearing aid (or cannot find it). I sat beside her because I know how much she treasures my company, but I have no interest in the antics being displayed on the screen and I was trying to work on my writing. I could have gone to sit in my bedroom, but then she would have felt snubbed. Still, it was hard for me to sit there with all that noise. I have often told her that I like silence, but she doesn't believe me. From time to time she asked if I would like the television turned off, and I said that it was fine as long as she watched it and allowed me to work. But every minute or two she made a comment and demanded a response from me: "Look at that woman's hair! See the beautiful flowers. Isn't this an old film?" and when I kept silent, she asked whether I had heard her. I would explain that I was fine with her watching and me working. It's just that she wanted to involve me in her activity, and I found this infuriating.

I was able to ignore the flickering and chattering of the television, but I could not ignore her voice. She would promise to be quiet and not interrupt me again, but she suffers increasingly from short-term memory loss. Looked at in one way, this is a blessing: She has reached a state that many of us are still aiming for in that she is more often than not in the present moment and does not refer back to the past. Still, for those around her, it does test the extent of their patience. As I often remark to my brother, my mother is more ecologically conscious than the rest of us, and she recycles her conversation every minute or so. Before I could get to the end of another sentence, she would be asking me innocently to look at the television again. Why did I find it so hard to give her this time? There is probably little of it enough left. I was trying to deny her my attention—the one thing that it is in my power to give but which I was selfishly withholding from her. Much of what she says and does these days is no longer under her control. I was ashamed of my lack of generosity and resolved not to tussle with her that way again. What on earth did I think I was achieving by punishing her in this way?

Gradually I became aware that it was simpler (and kinder, of course) to say yes to what was happening and let it be, to "suffer" it, in the real sense of the word. After that it was not nearly so hard to sit in the living room with her hour after hour, joining her in her activity rather than attempting to flee in my mind. After all, I had traveled three thousand miles to be with her. What was the point of wishing myself somewhere else?

Last night I was invited to accompany someone to a concert of art songs. I didn't quite grasp that all the songs had been commissioned especially for this performance, and indeed all the composers were present and took their bows. Much of the music was atonal (I think that is the right word). There were no tunes you could hum, i.e., not the kind of music I enjoy listening to. It all took a huge effort on the part of the performers and the audience. This was not a demand I wanted to respond to, particularly since the soprano soloist was large, enthusiastic, and didn't really need a microphone (there were moments when I had to put my hands over my ears to protect them from the inexorable, piercing sound). My first impulse was to escape, but we were right at the front and my companion would have been upset if I had walked out, so I decided that I had better stay put. I didn't try to blank out what was taking place on the stage. Instead, I looked for features of the performance that I could appreciate. It is a rare event that has absolutely nothing to recommend it. The two music directors, who were also the pianists and hosts for the evening, gave a superb performance in each of their roles. The singers were very accomplished. Possibly the composers were gifted also, even if their work didn't appeal to me. So it was not a total loss. I would certainly go to a concert organized by this group in the future—once I was sure that the music was at least a hundred years old. I was just unlucky in my choice of program.

Far too often in my life I have spent time imagining that other people are doing all kinds of wonderful things while I am home alone. This is another form of resistance—a refusal to be wherever you happen to be, doing whatever you happen to be doing. In fact, it is a double denial: You are not out there with the phantom revelers, and neither are you back here on your own.

I heard an interview the other day on National Public Radio with a tai chi instructor. He was describing how much more energy people feel they have once they start practicing tai chi. He always points out to them that what has occurred is that they are not using up so much of their energy tensing their bodies. Once you stop contracting your muscles unnecessarily, a great deal of energy is no longer being wasted.

The other side of offering no resistance is setting things up so that resistance doesn't arise in the first place. Once I had learned the rudiments of playing the piano, a young Dutch woman invited me to join her in a Mozart piece for four hands. Knowing that she was a skilled pianist, I panicked. First I explained that I was an absolute beginner and then that I couldn't sight-read, but she was not to be deterred. What I didn't know about her was that she was also an extraordinary teacher. We sat side by side at the keyboard, and she slowed her pace to my painful picking out of the notes. Each time I made a mistake, she would say, "Try stretching your finger a little farther" or "Yes, now play those two notes together." There was no hint of criticism in her demeanor. She supported me at every turn. Eventually we got to the end of a couple of pages of music, and she allowed me to escape. Both of us were all smiles. I don't remember the piece we played, but to this day I recall how she made me feel. She had only said "Yes." She never said "No." She taught by encouragement alone, and this allowed me to gradually drop all my fear and hesitation and enter into the spirit of the playing itself.

TEN

The Habit of Truth

I do not remember anyone instilling in me the importance of telling the truth, although I do recall how I explained it to Adam when he was small. I told him that not only was it the right thing to do but it was also the simplest. I could never understand why people lied. It seemed to me such a complicated way of operating. Once you had told someone something, you had to remember whom you had said what to and hope that this person would never interact with anyone to whom you had told a different tale. Those who lie appear to be setting themselves up for disaster, but perhaps the people who do it are unable to stop themselves.

The first time truthfulness was called into question for me was at boarding school when I was just four years old. After the customary afternoon nap, I had put on clean clothes and gone outside to play. I was watching several of the other girls drawing patterns in the dust with their white-socked feet when suddenly the headmistress appeared, and everyone scuttled to put their sandals back on. She asked the head girl, Georgina, who the culprits were, and I was identified as one of them. To this day I don't know whether this was because Georgina didn't like me, she wasn't sure who had been involved, or she thought that I had participated. Several of us were singled out, and while the rest of the group were sent off on that beautiful sunny afternoon to hunt for hens' eggs in the fields, we were taken to the gymnasium. There we were informed that because we liked taking our clothes off, we were now to take all of them off. (This was an ingenious form of making the punishment fit the crime.) Once this was done, we would be free to get dressed again and join the others outside. I remember that I was wearing a navy blue dress with a white Peter Pan collar and rows of little white elephants marching down to the hem. I stood there all afternoon, long after the other little girls had stripped, put their clothes back on, and gone off to play, because I adamantly refused to admit to a wrongdoing I hadn't committed. Even at that age truthfulness was of vital importance to me.

And in all these years I haven't shifted my position. My friends and acquaintances are often amused by how much of a stickler for the truth I am, but behind their smiles lurk both respect and relief. In business dealings they can rely on the fact that I will not fudge, that I will go out of my way to provide accurate details and correct any view that may lead to misunderstanding. They can also be sure that I will reveal things that may be to my disadvantage. I want them to have the full picture, believing that they are quite capable of drawing their own conclusions from what I tell them. And this is not something they can be sure of with most people. When I have discussed this with colleagues who also sell subsidiary rights, they give me the impression that they don't feel it is safe to give out this much information. They believe it will result in a less lucrative deal. I find this puzzling because as far as I can tell, I never got less money for something by doing this. I suspect that sometimes I got even more money than they might have because people find this way of doing business so refreshing.

In her poem "Ladder," Jane Hirshfield says, "Rarely are what is spoken and what is meant the same." I was astonished when I came across that line but on reflection realized that, indeed, this is unfortunately the case. Over the last decade there has been a degradation in the value of words. People no longer seem to have faith in the words of others, particularly anyone in public office or the press, and so they don't give what these people say any credence. And I have come to the reluctant conclusion that many people don't even understand what they themselves are saying. There is an imprecision that has crept into the language that is a little terrifying.

I try to be meticulous in my speech, in that I say exactly what I mean in the fewest possible words. From time to time I see that other people are taken aback by this forthrightness, because they are not used to it. There are certainly times when it is better to say nothing at all, but if you are going to speak, why not say what you mean? Get right to the point. Avoid the preamble. This doesn't mean that you have to be brutal.

You can cut to the chase and still be gentle, but it is a kindness to others not to hold back if there is really something you want to communicate. When I talk, there is no hidden agenda because nothing is hidden.

It is no secret that many English people find it hard to express a preference and are inclined to defer to the other person, not wishing to upset him or her in any way: "What would you like to do?" "Oh, I don't mind. What would you like to do?" "It doesn't matter to me, really. Would you like to go to a movie?" "Would you?" This exchange can go on for some time and even when it is over, neither English person is quite sure whether the final choice is mutually satisfying. Better to be clear in the beginning and get on to the next thing. Someone called today to ask me if I would like to go and see *Gladiator*, since it had just won an Oscar. I was pleased that I had been invited, but my answer was brief and to the point: "No, thank you. Go with someone else. I saw *Quo Vadis* when I was a teenager, and that is enough Roman stuff for me." If you say something this straight, other people know exactly where you stand.

I recall the broadcast that Saddam Hussein made to the American people during the Gulf War. It went on for a very long time, and almost no one could grasp his message because he never seemed to say whatever it was he wanted us all to know. All I took away from listening to it was the phrase "the mother of all battles" and the impression that Arabic was an even more indirect language than I had thought. I couldn't tell whether his style was more flowery and oblique than other Iraqis', but I suspect that it was. And this was sad because I think that many of us were curious to understand his point of view.

Telling the truth is completely uncomplicated; you don't have to work out any strategy. You just tell it like it is. Also, there is no residue. You don't find yourself wondering if you should or shouldn't have said something. This saves an inordinate amount of time and energy (two things at a premium these days).

Straight talk is vital when it comes to children. I learned this lesson when I was taking care of Lorraine. I had warned her that if she misbehaved in a certain way again (I no longer recall the circumstances), I would put her across my knee and spank her. When I said this, it was just a threat, and I thought it would be enough to deter her, particularly since she was at that time about seventeen. But then she disobeyed me once more, and I was honor bound to deliver. I applied a hairbrush ten times to her rump. When it was over there were tears in her eyes and I was taken aback, but I thought that perhaps the indignity had upset her. I hadn't struck her hard at all. About a year later she told me that it was not the punishment itself that had hurt so much but the quality of my attention. She said that anyone else would have brought the brush down in a different spot each time but because I was so careful, I hit her repeatedly in the same place and almost broke the skin. The moral of this story is not that I recommend corporal punishment. I don't. What is important here is that you shouldn't tell a child that you will do something (or not do something) unless you mean it, because, if you don't follow through and it is an empty promise, the child will no longer believe you or have any respect for you. (The same is true for adults, of course.) I know a woman who is always lashing out at her children verbally, but they no longer pay much attention to what she says because they know that she is speaking from anger and that she has no intention of fulfilling her threats.

Intimately connected to this is the practice of asking a child to do something when you yourself act differently. Children learn through mimicry and osmosis.

They copy the way you behave. If you are always anxious, the chances are that they will learn to be anxious too. It's in the air. If you remain calm, then they will not panic. You are the one providing the cues.

It follows that using reverse psychology also sends children a hollow message, and the repercussions later in their lives may be irreversible. And, last, I don't subscribe to the "If you eat one more mouthful, then you may . . ." school. Bargaining with children is an unfortunate practice. I admit that I was tempted to use both these methods when Adam was little, but I didn't succumb. I found that if I spoke with enough authority and really meant what I said, he heard me and would fall into line.

At one time in my life I was put in charge of the advertising for the philosophy school. I was instructed that all I needed to do was present what we were offering accurately and concisely, never promising that any particular result would come from trying it. After all, how could one know what the result might be for other people? The point of advertising is to offer customers goods and services they might need. It is not about tempting them to buy something they might want. There is a vast difference between necessity and desire.

I don't think that anyone remembers this anymore. Copywriters nowadays imagine that their job is to arouse desire. They do this by pinpointing a perceived need, but it is rarely a true need.

The first person we have to tell the truth to is ourselves. If we are not going to be honest with ourselves, there is little possibility that we will treat anyone else differently. This is a thorny issue. I sometimes sweep everything under the rug by saying "Perhaps I am naïve . . ." when I don't want to admit that I have been foolish enough to hoodwink myself. I pretend that someone else has seduced me into seeing it her or his way but if I went along with it, then the responsibility was mine just as much as the other person's. Time and again the evidence is right in front of me, and yet I choose to ignore it. I may call it "giving someone the benefit of the doubt," but we all know that this is often a reluctance to face the facts. We prefer to believe the illusion we have laid over the situation. We need to look at our relationships with other people as well as our relationship with ourselves. Both are generally a little murky.

Many people felt that my marriage was a mistake (and some were unkind enough to tell me so. Honesty is fine when it is called for, but kindness should temper full disclosure.). When our marriage fell apart, these people were quick to blame my husband—which was unfortunate. I don't believe that he was any more at fault than I was. We both chose not to see certain things in ourselves and in each other. Like many couples, we put on blindfolds when we fell in love. Years later when he was in therapy, he said to me, "I am just coming out of my cave. When we were married, I didn't even know I was in a cave." I had never met anyone who lived in a psychological cave. He certainly seemed more private than anyone I had been close to, but I had put it down to shyness. I thought that once we were living together, that would fall away. But people are the way they are, and they don't change just because they move in together—at least, not in my experience. What you see is what you get. The other person may not be seeing you very clearly, so you need to be certain that you see who he or she is.

While I was typing the last paragraph, I received a call from a man in Florida who had courted me shortly after the breakup of my marriage. He had called me out of the blue two days ago, saying that he had been sorting through some of his papers and had come across my name. It transpired that his own marriage had now fallen apart, and when he saw my name he recalled the feelings he had had for me and felt impelled to get in touch. We talked for a little while, and I was as free and easy with him as I had been all those years ago. When he called just now he told me that he had been thinking of me very warmly for the last two days and he was wondering . . . You can imagine the rest of the conversation without my filling you in. I told him that I was happy for us to be friends but that it could not go any further than that. I had refused him over twenty years ago (I had told him gently that I could not marry anyone without a sense of humor), and the situation hadn't changed. He was sad. He had been building up this whole picture in the interval between Monday and Wednesday. All I could do was read him what I had written in the last paragraph and point out that it applied to me, to Neil, but also to him. We have to face the truth.

There are certain sentences and phrases that really hit home when you first hear them, and then continue to reverberate throughout your life. For me, one of the most powerful is the statement in Isaiah 43: "Ye are my witnesses, saith the Lord." *Witness* is a strong word, and nowadays we tend to think of a witness as someone who observes dispassionately. The original meaning of the word is much deeper. The root is the Anglo-Saxon *witan*, "to know," from which we get the expression "to have your wits about you." So witnessing has to do with transparency, seeing through the scrim that generally covers things and looking deeply into them so that we know and understand what they truly are. When God says, "Ye are my witnesses," it means that the role of human beings is to know divinity and to know it now. The sentence is in the present tense. We are here to see and experience God in all things. Or, as Kabir Helminski describes it in his book *A Knowing Heart: A Sufi Path of Transformation*: "The true human being embodies the divine presence."

So often we see only what we want to see. Our desires get in the way of our observation, and we look at part of something rather than all of it or we distort what is right in front of us in other ways. Everyone wears different glasses—metaphorically speaking—and has a different prescription. Some people have an astigmatism (I do). Some like to wear tinted glasses. And then there are those who like to wear dark glasses or shades. Presumably they like to look on the gloomy side.

When I was growing up, history was taught as though the account we were given was the only view. Many years later, when I started working at Knopf, which had a fine American history list, I gradually came to the realization that there could be as many views of what took place at a battle as the number of soldiers who fought in it, not to mention all those who reported from the front or wrote about it later. One of the most honest titles for a memoir I have come across is Nicolas Bentley's *A Version of the Truth*. Nick was a cartoonist and also an editor at André Deutsch. He understood that no perspective is complete. So much of the time we see things a certain way because of our background and experience, and we fail to grasp that what we are aware of is only one of a multitude of possibilities. In addition, all of us interpret (or misinterpret) circumstances differently. Each of us focuses on different facets and glosses over what doesn't interest us or those things we would prefer to avoid (whether this is something we are willing to admit or not). Consequently, everyone formulates an individual picture of what is happening. No two people inhabit precisely the same spot on the planet.

This became even clearer to me when I was attending an art class and the week's assignment was to draw the same object each day from a different angle. I was astonished to look at the variety that appeared in my sketchbook. The following week we were asked to focus just on the spaces described by the object we had chosen and record them on the paper. I was again fascinated at how different a chair seemed when I drew the gaps between the decorative woodwork slats on the back, then the trapezoid shapes caused by the legs, and finally the edge of the enormous space surrounding the whole chair. The third week we were told to choose a photograph of a familiar object and turn it upside down before we drew it. It is extraordinary how this transforms your view.

These three exercises revolutionized the way I saw the world. As I write this I am sitting outside my friend Lynn's house in New Jersey, observing the slivers of the next-door garden visible between the trunks of the trees at the edge of her property. Normally, I would focus on the adjacent garden and ignore the trees in the foreground. My mind would fill in what was hidden from view with what could reasonably be expected to be there. The trees themselves would vanish from existence, because subliminally I considered them to be an obstruction. Now that I remember that art class, however, I see the blocks of space between the trunks and branches which all slope in different directions—a geometrical profusion of possibilities. I become aware of the distance between me and the trees, and also of the grass and bushes and wildflowers, the play of sunlight and shadow, the unseen area behind my back, the invisible birds calling to one another in their liquid language, the rustling leaves, and the fading drone of an airplane in the sky. My perspective shifts with each of these acknowledgments, and my appreciation of the garden expands. But, of course, the ant scurrying past my foot is probably unaware of most of this, yet cognizant of a whole universe I shall never know.

It is good to bear all this in mind when you read or listen to other people's stories. Recognize that while they may believe that what they are telling you is the facts, their "truth" undoubtedly comes from a limited viewpoint.

This is probably as good a place as any to make a disclaimer about the stories I tell in this book: I have not knowingly distorted anything, but as I grow older my memory is increasingly unreliable. If those who appear in my stories remember the circumstances differently, I hope they will forgive me. What I describe here is the way I perceived things at the time they happened, but, of course, I was looking only from my own point of view, and, in addition, much time may have elapsed in the interim.

Here is the way that Jungian analyst Helen Luke describes the process in her book *Old Age*. She reimagines Hermes speaking to Odysseus on his final journey of "a spirit of discriminating wisdom, separating moment by moment the wheat of life from the chaff, so that you may know in both wheat and chaff their meaning and their value in the pattern of the universe."

Nowadays many people no longer understand what it means to discriminate. They think that it is choosing one thing over another, but, in fact, discrimination is as Helen Luke describes it: recognizing exactly what's what; not being confused about the nature of things. Adultery happens not just between consenting adults.

To adulterate is to mix things so that they are no longer pure, whether the substance is metal, food, or the present moment. In fact, if you remain in the present and avoid impurity now by not importing the past or the future, then the chances are that nothing will spill over and contaminate other moments.

ELEVEN

What Nourishes Us

Whatever we put into our bodies, minds, and hearts is what feeds them; but I am not sure that we appreciate the implications of this, and we are often very careless about what we consume. We think, "Oh, it's just this once," but these "onces" become habitual and can soon add up to a lifetime of neglect.

Our life depends on the air we breathe, yet we draw air into our lungs without really considering where it is coming from and what it will do to us. We know the difference it makes when the air is crystal clear and we take deep drafts of it as we stride across the fields. We feel invigorated, and everything around us sparkles.

Contrast this with how we feel in a stuffy train or office where the air is recycled and who knows when there will be any new oxygen available. The mind becomes dull and the body sluggish. More and more places are suffering from air pollution because neither the authorities nor the population take the consequences of their actions seriously. I was recently in Shanghai, a city of thirteen million with a floating population of another three million itinerant construction workers, and I learned that all the children there are already affected by the polluted quality of the air, caused by heavy traffic.

When I grew up in England, everyone kept their windows open a little, no matter how cold or wet it was. We believed that the way to remain healthy was to keep the air circulating and allow fresh air to enter the house at all times. I still believe this and shut my windows only on those rare days when fierce winds cause grit to accumulate on the windowsills. I can't honestly say whether it is because I have a strong constitution, I eat a healthy diet, or because the air in my home is always fresh, but I rarely suffer from colds and flu the way other people seem to. In addition to breathing fresh air in our homes, we need to get out every day and walk vigorously, so that our blood doesn't start to curdle. This will do wonders for our constitution and doesn't cost nearly as much as membership in a health club.

We also need to be careful what we drink. I don't subscribe to the school of thought that says we should imbibe eight glasses of water a day. Each person needs a different amount of liquid, depending on her or his build and activities. For many years all I drank was three cups of strong coffee a day and perhaps a few mouthfuls of water at lunch, but on reflection I don't think that this was a very wise habit and I am lucky that my body didn't rebel. I do know that drinking a great deal of anything during a meal is harmful to the digestion because it dilutes the digestive juices both in our mouths and in our stomachs. I prefer to drink either before or after a meal, and I have found that my system prefers it too. I also drink only when I am thirsty. Whatever your favorite beverage is, take a moment to consider how much of it you drink each day (be honest) and what the cumulative effect of this consumption may be.

A simple and delicious way to eat is to choose food that is as close to its natural state as you can find and then enjoy it without adding or taking anything away from it, that is, without cooking or seasoning. Lanza del Vasto described it as "putting as little space and time as possible between the earth and your mouth." Choose fruits and vegetables that are fresh and in season and that have not traveled too long or too far before you buy them. If you can discover fruit that has ripened on the tree and was not sprayed in the process, so much the better. Then eat it at its best, with the taste of the sun still there. Resist the temptation to garnish everything, and you will find that an avocado, if it is a good avocado, has a flavor all its own. In fact, each avocado (or apple or apricot) seems to taste completely different from any other you have ever eaten.

From time to time I stock up my shelves with dried herbs; beans in all colors, shapes, and sizes; and a variety of grains, cookies, and crackers. They form a wonderful display in their glass jars, but months go by and I forget to use any of them. What I actually consume are the things in my short-term memory—whatever I have bought in the last few days. I go to the fruit and vegetable market and buy whatever is fresh and firm (beware of produce that is bruised or flabby). I am, after all, the granddaughter of a Covent Garden wholesale fruit and vegetable merchant. I do not buy more than I can use within two or three days because then it will no longer be fresh. This is hard to stick to when I visit a farmers' market because there is so much wonderful stuff, but you have to be stern with yourself and buy with your head and not your belly. I also find it difficult to restrain myself when it comes to quantities of wondrous-looking fruit and vegetables. When I am putting them into plastic bags, I have to remind myself to buy enough for only one dish. This is particularly hard when I am cooking just for myself. But I believe that it is a crime to take home more than I can use.

When the moment comes to prepare a meal, I look in the refrigerator and see what is there and what combination of foods seems right for the day and hour. This is just the way I choose what to wear in the morning. The resulting meals (and outfits) can be quite stunning if you don't have preconceived ideas of what goes together and what doesn't. It is not that I never use cookbooks, but I tend to use them for inspiration rather than information. If I have someone coming to dinner, I occasionally consult a cookbook. I leaf all the way through and always come up with a recipe that includes ingredients that are not in season. This is because we are always attracted by something unavailable (or, at least, I am). Then I try to figure out how I can adapt the recipe I have chosen for ingredients that I can actually find.

Even if you have a large family, try to estimate quantities accurately. Almost everyone would prefer a new dish rather than leftovers day after day. Yes, I know that nowadays there are such things as freezers, and people are always encouraging me to make enough for several meals and tuck portions away in the deep freeze. But psychologically this does not work for me. I just can't believe that eating food that is canned, bottled, dried, or frozen is as good as eating produce that is only a few hours old. Of course it is possible to survive by eating foods that have had all these things done to them, but over the long haul I suspect that they take their toll. You can also be nourished by foods already prepared and available in stores; however, you will be far more nourished by food you have prepared yourself, and it will also be cheaper and simpler.

I well remember going home to England shortly after I had become a strict vegetarian. My mother had saved the first fruit and vegetables of the season so that she could offer them to me when I visited her, but she had frozen each and every one. I adamantly refused to eat any of them, even though she claimed that they were "freshly frozen." I have relaxed quite a bit since those days. I am no longer a complete vegetarian, and when I am in someone else's house, I do my best to eat what is put in front of me. It probably won't kill me, I may never go to heaven (being a vegetarian is probably not a good enough reason for ending up there), and it is rude and unkind to make a fuss if you are a guest unless the food is going to make you ill.

At one period in my life, I ate everything raw except for bread and cheese, and I also ate only one thing at a time. I shared an apartment in an old Federal house in the Village with two other women, and we would bake our own bread and put an extraordinary selection of fruit, vegetables, cheese, nuts, and honey on the table every day. Whatever we had in the house was offered at every meal. This simple diet is not as boring as it may sound because the variety is constantly changing. Visitors were wide-eyed at the cornucopia.

Each of us would choose what to eat by consulting our stomachs. Generally we carry around some idea about what we would like to eat, but it is often a desire we have been nurturing for some time. If you sit at the table and actually ask your body what it wants, the answer may surprise you. So you might start with some cherries. You would put on your plate only as many cherries as you were sure you could eat. When you had finished them, you could certainly take more or you could move on to something else, but you couldn't combine foods except with bread, i.e., bread and cheese or bread and honey. This measured way of eating gives your body just what it needs at any given meal, and there are never any leftovers.

Perhaps you are wondering how this works with children? In my house it worked very well. I provided a large selection at every meal, and Adam could pick anything he wanted from what was there. Because everything was already on the table, he was not tempted to ask for something else because he knew we didn't have it. Children like a choice, just as we all do, and they should be given the freedom to make it. Having in the house only foods I believed would be good for him meant that he exercised his choice from what was available and I never had to say "No."

Eating like this simplifies life enormously. The food is quick and easy to prepare (most of it just needs washing or arranging on a plate), there are no pots and pans to cope with afterward, and when you rise from the table, you never feel weighed down.

I no longer eat this way (except occasionally when I am lunching at home alone) although I really like it, but if you have never tried it, do experiment with it a little. It really fine-tunes your ability to recognize and respond to what your body actually needs. The way most of us tend to eat is by putting a lot on our plates and confusing our taste buds by putting two or more things in our mouths at the same time. Keep in mind that if fruit and vegetables are not in a good enough condition to eat raw—if they have no taste or are not yet ripe—adorning them with a sauce or adding flavoring other than salt is not going to benefit you or your stomach. Nowadays I cook my vegetables by steaming, stir-frying, or roasting them in the oven with a little olive oil, and I keep the cooking time to a minimum.

I have focused on fruit, vegetables, and grains because they are the foundation of what I eat, but much of what I have said also applies to meat and fish. The principles are what are important here.

One thing that may change your attitude toward food is saying grace. In 1992, Bell Tower published a little book by Marcia and Jack Kelly entitled *One Hundred Graces*. In the introduction I wrote about the function and nature of mealtime blessings:

Saying grace is an ancient and vital tradition the world over. To begin with, it provides a space, a moment of stillness, in which to relinquish the activities of the day, and allow the mind to settle. Then, as we acknowledge the source of our nourishment, we are filled with astonishment at the generosity of the Creator, with gratitude, and with praise. In bringing the body, mind, and heart together, we come to ourselves, and remember who we are and why we are here. For some families, a meal is the only time everyone is present and so the opportunity to enjoy one another and really celebrate the occasion is not to be lost. For many, a meal is also the only time that there is any memory of the Divine. Saying grace establishes an immediate connection with that memory. In such a moment, when our minds are clear and the truth is reinforced by being sounded aloud, we can dedicate the meal and the strength we receive from it to the service of whoever or whatever is before us.

Once you have the food in front of you (cooked or raw), the next thing is to remember to taste every mouthful; otherwise, it is such a waste. How many times have you wolfed something down because it was your favorite food and realized when your plate was empty that you did not actually taste any of it? So smell it, taste it, chew it, and swallow it only when you are sure you have experienced it.

I am not going to talk about smoking or taking drugs because I have little experience of the former and absolutely none of the latter. I have never found either habit appealing, and I cannot believe that introducing these substances into our bodies can be beneficial in the long run.

During my pregnancy I amassed a few books on child care that I trusted would stand me in good stead for the first few years of my baby's life. I was ill for most of the nine months and did not feel like focusing on how to cope once the pregnancy was over. Once Adam arrived, there never seemed any time to read, so the books remained almost untouched on my shelf until he grew up. I did consult Dr. Spock once but wasn't thrilled to discover that he offered three solutions to whatever the problem was. I had been expecting just one foolproof answer, and I never tried Spock again.

However, I got the very best advice one day from a huge black grandmother sitting next to me on the Broadway bus. I don't know how we got into conversation, but to this day I can hear her telling me that the most important thing you can do for a boy is give him his independence as early as possible. What she said went right in and stayed there.

I wasn't one of those mothers who fret about their children when they leave them at home with someone else. I stayed home for the first seven weeks, but Neil was out of a job, and, to be honest, I itched to get back to the office. So I started work again quickly. I worked at home three days a week and on the other two days went in to the office from 10 A.M. to 3 P.M. I found a friend with a small child. She was willing to earn some extra money by coming to my house to look after both her child and my own two days a week, and that left me free for a few hours. It never occurred to me that disaster could strike in my absence, and Adam tended not to notice that I was leaving. I kept up this schedule for a year, but after the first six months, he was so active that it was hard for me to get any work done at home. He wanted to be out in the park running around, and I felt tied to the telephone during office hours.

So then I found a wonderful West Indian woman who had a raft of children of her own. She came to my house every day, enabling me to go back to the office full-time, and Adam would often go home with her for the weekend and sleep in a big bed with several other kids if I had to be away for some reason. People regarded me with some horror, I think, because when I left town, I didn't call every day to find out how Adam was and speak to him. I reckoned that he was probably fine. If he wasn't fine, she would let me know. After all, I had left him with a woman I trusted completely. It seemed to me that calling him all the time would remind him of my absence, and he was better off without this thought.

Once I returned to work, the most difficult moment was coming home in the evening. As I walked through the door, both Adam and Miss Grace, our blue-gray Persian cat, would fling themselves at me, wanting both food and affection. There was no chance to sit down for a while and catch my breath. I talked to Ram Dass about this, and he pointed out that I was teaching Adam how to come home and deal with whatever the situation was without missing a beat or losing my temper. This was an important lesson he might not learn during the "quality" time I never seemed to have an opportunity to spend with him.

Just how quickly independence took over became very clear on Adam's first day at preschool. When I returned from work, I was anxious to know how everything had gone. (You guessed right: I was not one of those mothers who hovered in the wings for the first day. I took him to the front door and simply handed him over with a hug.) So I asked him to tell me what he had done.

"Ate cheese sandwich," was the only response I got. Because I myself had made this cheese sandwich, his eating it was not a great surprise. I was curious to know about everything else, but he either couldn't or wouldn't tell me. Perhaps the cheese sandwich was the high point of his day. It was then that I realized that never again would I know what he was up to all day. But he was fine. He was enjoying everything, and now he had lots of company to play with and learn from.

Although motherhood was the most exhausting experience of my life, it was also the most rewarding. The strength of the bond that I felt with Adam was something I had never anticipated. And then there were all those moments that are etched into my memory forever.

I remember him asking me one afternoon when he was a year or so older, "Does God have a birthday every day?"

I wasn't sure where he had picked up this idea, but I liked it.

"Yes," I responded. "I think you could say that he does. He creates everything new every day."

"And does Mrs. God celebrate his birthday with him?" Adam asked next.

God, it seemed, was often on his mind. There was another occasion the same year, when he was six. This time he wanted to know:

"Why didn't God interfere when they were trying to kill his son?"

"God doesn't interfere. He just makes the rules and watches to see what happens" was the best I could manage. (Why didn't Dr. Spock have some ready answers for this kind of question?)

"I would have interfered," Adam announced.

"So would I, if someone tried to kill you," I said.

"It's a shame Jesus didn't become an angel before he died" was his next remark. This was a little bewildering. I wondered where he was going with this one.

"Why do you think he should have become an angel?"

"Because he was such a nice man," Adam replied. I had never heard Jesus described this way, but it was probably true. Still, I was curious:

"What makes you say that?" I asked.

"He always wore a sun on his head" came the answer.

Finally, there was a conversation about death. I don't think that any of us are ever ready for this, but we do our best. We were walking down Broadway one day when he asked me what happens when we die.

"No one really knows," I responded, "but many people believe that first you have a rest with God for a little while and then you come back here and live another life."

"I'm not coming back," he announced with some conviction.

"Well, I don't really think you have a choice," I offered, no longer certain of my ground.

"You mean I may have to come back, whether I want to or not?" said Adam. And that is where we left it.

It became increasingly clear to me that not only does a baby in the womb use all a mother's resources—literally feeding on her body—but this process also continues throughout childhood. A mother provides nourishment for her child at every level, whether she is aware of it or not. Some of this food may be good and some not so good, but everything that she thinks, feels, says, and does affects her offspring as well as her. There is no holding any of it back. It is an open system.

When he was about nine years old, he told me that he wanted to come home from school on his own. He felt too old to be met by a baby-sitter every day. I would walk him to school in the morning before I went to work. I would take him as far as Seventy-eighth Street and West End Avenue and watch as he crossed the street and entered the gate of Collegiate School. In my heart I would say good-bye to him, knowing that there is never any guarantee that we will see our loved ones again, although we always count on doing so.

I was comfortable (well, almost) with the idea of

his walking home on his own. I had taught him not just to check the traffic lights before he crossed the street but to watch the eyes of the drivers of each car. I explained that some drivers weren't very awake and you could not always count on the fact that they would obey the lights. But if you observed them carefully, you could easily tell what they were planning to do.

Neil freaked out when I told him that Adam was now making his own way home, but I explained firmly that this was New York and the sooner Adam learned how to be self-reliant the safer he would be.

As it turned out, only one incident occurred on the way home, and it was about a year later. I was very proud of the way Adam handled it. He was walking up Broadway where there were always lots of people, and several boys he did not know jumped him and ran off with his backpack. He chased them down the block and eventually, I think, they abandoned his backpack because it was so heavy. Then he went to the nearest phone and called the police to report what had happened, before walking the rest of the way home.

How we choose to feed our minds is just as important as what we put into our bodies. At every moment of the day we are receiving impressions through sight, sound, smell, taste, and touch. If we are deprived of these sensations, we start to feel disembodied. So we need to take a fresh look at everything we are inviting into our minds.

It is no secret these days that older people who keep learning new things enjoy themselves and live longer than those who don't. In addition to stretching the mind with some form of study (it doesn't have to be something new, but it is good to keep the mind engaged in intellectual pursuit), have a look at the books you read, the art and sculpture you admire, the music you listen to, and so on. Spectator sports such as football and the Internet are fine occasionally, but we need to watch that they do not become a steady diet so that we forget to eat anything else.

On subways and buses when I am forced to share some of the music other people are listening to because their headphones are leaking, I worry about what such an insistent beat and screech is doing to their brains. Some music appeals to our sense of rhythm, some to our emotions, and some to our intelligence, and we need to make sure that none of these three is being starved. There are times when I realize that I have spent too long in front of the computer screen and I am all in my head. This is the moment for me to put on some Cuban music and dance myself loose for a little while, but I wouldn't dream of listening to this music all the time. There needs to be a balance here as in all things. There are times when I yearn for Mozart or Hildegard of Bingen, and there are times when I don't.

Again, I am concerned when people I know spend a lot of time watching horror or action movies. I go to the movies to be moved (isn't that why they are called "movies"?), either to tears or laughter. I don't want to be shocked or scared for entertainment. There is enough of that in real life.

Then there is conversation. How rare it is these days to participate in a real conversation. So much of what we share with our friends is gossip, complaints, conjecture, or reminiscence, and none of this is nourishing in the least. For three years I hosted a monthly meeting for friends and acquaintances for whom this kind of talk was no longer enough. We gathered together for a couple of hours, beginning with a short meditation and then proceeding to an open discussion of "what really matters." There was no set theme, no one was in charge, and once someone had begun to speak we all listened carefully without interrupting. The one rule we had was that during this short and precious time we wouldn't talk of anything else. Just once a month we attempted to devote at least two hours to speaking the truth.

We all need good company, friends we can depend on for spiritual sustenance. It is not always possible to meet on a regular basis the way we did, but everyone needs friends and relations who will always be there for them and vice versa.

Each day it is good to set aside some time for nourishing the body with exercise, the mind with reading and contemplating scripture or wisdom teachings, and the spirit with some form of devotion such as meditation or prayer. These things are as vital to us as a whole person as those foods with which we choose to feed our bodies. For each person, the timetable for doing this will be different, but I have found that starting the day with yoga before breakfast, and meditation and reading afterward, is a good preparation for everything that lies ahead. Then, again, in the evening, it is good to preface it with more exercise (in my case, tai chi chuan) and meditation so that there is a clear separation from the workday. The quality of what we feed ourselves on every level will manifest itself in our lives and in our relationships with other people.

TWELVE

A Balancing Act

Nowadays most of us feel as though we are being dragged along at breakneck speed in directions we would really rather not go. Somehow we need to find a way of slowing down, stepping off this path, and reestablishing a balance in our lives. It might be helpful to think of it as reeducation in that it is not as though we need to introduce something new. We already have what it takes. It has just become a little buried, and we need to lead it out to pasture again. The Latin root of *educate* does indeed mean "leading out." We need to slough off the accumulation of so many of the cultural ideas we have acquired over the years.

Balance has to do with remaining in the moment, neither looking back wistfully nor looking too far forward. The not-looking-back is a lot easier for some people than others. I happen to be one of those lucky people who don't miss other people and objects once I am no longer in their presence. This may be because I went away to boarding school at a very early age and felt compelled to learn self-sufficiency. I don't know. What I do know is that this sometimes causes distress to my mother. Every time I fly back to New York, she says, "I'll miss you. Will you miss me?" And I tell her that I wish she would not ask that, because she knows that I rarely miss people. My answer can only upset her. If I am with people, fine, but if not, so be it. I don't like to be torn between two realities.

The same goes for looking too far forward. I try not to think about what may happen at some event that I hope to go to. You never know these days. Maybe you'll get there but maybe you won't. There is an infinite number of possibilities in any given moment, but we endeavor to control our destiny most of the time.

The older I get, the less set in stone things seem to be. If I don't have expectations that are too high, I will not be disappointed.

For instance, when I knew that a friend from northern California was going to be in New York, I purchased tickets for a film festival. Later I discovered that she had changed her dates and would no longer be in town that day. I was disconcerted, but I invited another friend to go with me. Then, a few days before the event, I had to fly to London to be with my mother, who had suffered a stroke. I mailed both tickets to my New York friend, and she asked someone else to accompany her. At the last minute she herself fell ill and had to give both tickets to her friend. Luckily, neither she nor I had anything but mild regret over what had happened.

Living in the present doesn't mean that you can't or shouldn't plan ahead. You need to have an intention in mind when you embark on something, but the thing to do is make plans and then wait to see what happens. There are no guarantees. For instance, last fall I gathered seeds from both the red and the pink hollyhocks in our community garden, and I sowed them all along the edge of the path. I had this vision of an army of old-fashioned blossoms guarding the path like sentinels. Now that it is early summer I am watching to see if any or all of them will come up. Life is just like this. You can sow all kinds of seeds but you never know which ones will germinate or what will befall any of them once they sprout.

Another way of allowing more freedom into the mind is not holding fixed ideas about people and things. This is a tough one. Over the years we observe how other people behave in certain situations, and we come to the conclusion that they will always react in the same way. But in our heart of hearts, we know this is not true. For instance, I have built up a picture of one of the doormen in my building as being an old curmudgeon, someone who never does the right thing. It is true that ever since he had a heart attack his behavior has been erratic, but he means well most of the time, and the fact that I carry around this negative idea most probably produces the result I expect.

I once published a book by Jean Liedloff called *The Continuum Concept,* which described how children almost without exception do what you expect them to do. If you are afraid that they will fall into the fishpond, they will. Just keep the idea in your mind. You don't have to say anything out loud. Children have an uncanny ability to connect with what you are thinking and feeling rather than what you may be saying. Your mind is the environment in which they dwell. In the years when I was bringing up my son, I expected him to go to bed when I asked him to, and he always did. I myself had always gone to bed when I was told to when I was small. It did not occur to me that Adam would not go willingly to bed and then to sleep, and so it did not occur to him either. I had a theory that the reason so many American children seemed to have problems at bedtime was that the parents were not sure whether the children would go to bed, and so the children were not sure either: i.e., the parents created the problem in the first place.

What I am suggesting here is that we hold neither positive nor negative ideas, that we try to stay as present as possible and just see what happens. I know this is hard, particularly if you have a history with a friend who seems to cancel or postpone every appointment you make. But if you can bring yourself to do this, both you and the friend will taste a wonderful freedom in your relationship with each other.

Lately I have become very aware of the way we introduce stress into our speech, particularly in New York City. It is almost as though we are beating time as we speak. We come down stronger on some parts of a sentence than others. We probably think of it as "emphasis," but it is a very different way of speaking than is customary, say, in England. If you listen to an English person say "the White House" or "the weekend," you will notice that all the syllables have the same weight. They are evenly balanced. Yet in this country we put the stress on the first syllable, and the second one is almost insignificant. I suspect that we have built the stress we are all experiencing into the very way we speak.

Those people whose voices are most restful are those who do not add this push. You can hold people's attention more easily if you neither drop nor raise your voice at the end of each sentence. Your audience is left hanging on your words. It is a fascinating phenomenon. Your voice floats on the air, and people's minds have less of a tendency to get carried off into their own trains of thought. One person who seems to understand this is Toni Packer from the Springwater Center for Meditative Inquiry near Rochester, New York. I was on a retreat with her, and once a day she gave a short talk (the retreat was otherwise silent). Her words and phrases came and went, the sound of her voice never falling at the end of each sentence, so that we all felt gentled, then released, and borne aloft like milk-weed parachutes drifting up and away.

The way to walk the middle path in relation to money is not so very different. You need to find a way to stay balanced.

I have never made a concerted effort to make money but I was brought up during World War II, and it comes naturally to me to be frugal. So anything I don't really need, I don't acquire (well, of course, sometimes I slip from this, but I have to make a real effort!). When any money accumulates in my checking account, I either give it to a good cause or salt it away somewhere. When I salt it away, I make sure that it doesn't just sit there. I treat it like one of the plants on my windowsill. I water it and watch it carefully, waiting for it to grow. If nothing seems to be happening after a reasonable amount of time, I repot it. This is the method I use for investing, and it has served me well.

Although I was a single parent for most of the period during which Adam was growing up, I managed to pay all his school bills without taking out a loan and emerged at the other end with a tidy sum still in the account.

I remember one year in the 1970s when I earned $12,500, and the man I was working for earned $100,000 (I knew this because we were trying to get his tax return in on time). I had saved money out of my pittance and he hadn't, but of course he had two more wives to support than I did. What I am trying to say is that I don't save money in order to save it. It gets saved because I don't spend it as often as other people seem to.

It is really a question of how you view money. I don't make a budget, but perhaps on some level there's a budget in the back of my mind. I don't allocate a specific sum for this or that. If I need something, I always look for the best quality as well as the best value. If I don't really need something, I simply don't buy it.

Although the best quality is often the most expensive, in the long run this usually works out cheaper. The writer Laurie Colwin once took me down to Canal

Street, where she frequented secondhand-clothes shops on a regular basis. She was astonished to find that I had never been to one. I trotted around after her all Saturday morning and by the time we sat down to lunch in a café, she was in despair, but I was elated and amused. She felt as though the whole expedition had been a failure. I had watched her buy a dun-colored cashmere cardigan for twenty-five dollars because she admired the buttons. In my opinion, the color was so awful, I couldn't imagine ever choosing to put it on. If this was the case, why spend twenty-five dollars for the buttons? At one point she took me to a store where they had a sale on men's alpaca overcoats. The coats were luscious, and I tried one on. Not surprisingly, it hung on me, making me look like a dwarf. She bunched handfuls of the silky cloth behind my back to show me how it would look if I had it altered, but I pointed out to her that the whole coat would have to be remade to fit me and so in the end it would cost far more than if I bought a coat that was the right size. In addition, I didn't need a new winter coat.

I told her that I had really enjoyed accompanying her because I thought that perhaps I had been missing something by not visiting thrift shops, and now I knew that I had not. Also, it made my heart feel glad to have seen all those clothes and not bought any. I felt as though I had saved a fortune. I was not at all disappointed. I explained to her that I wouldn't be surprised if I spent less money on clothes than she did even though what I normally did was buy good-quality garments in classic styles. I considered clothes to be a kind of investment. I bought the best, only if and when there was a need, in styles that I knew suited me, and then expected them to last for twenty years. She, on the other hand, sallied forth every week and bought something cheap that might or might not go with garments already in her wardrobe. I would have been curious to tally up what each of us spent over the year, but I didn't want to push her too far. Also, of course, she was using shopping as a form of entertainment, and I was not.

I have to admit that there is one aspect of spending where I often get hooked, and that is with mail-order catalogs. These, of course, arrive in avalanches, but I have learned to distinguish at a glance which ones have clothes in natural—not man-made—fabrics that suit me (nothing tight; there must be plenty of room for movement). Mail order is less exhausting than traipsing around stores, and if you can discover a couple of catalogs that offer merchandise you are consistently happy with, buying this way is a real boon.

I tend to go through my favorite catalogs almost as soon as they arrive in the mail (if you wait too long, the things you want are often no longer available in your size). I turn down the corners of the pages of my selections, and I put the catalog aside for a little while. Catalogs are very seductive, and the only way to deal with them is not to pick up the phone immediately. Exercise restraint. Look at the catalog again about a week later and be honest with yourself: Will you actually wear what looks so splendid on the page or will it lurk in your closet for the next few years, haunting you each time you peer in? When exactly would you wear it? Once I have examined my conscience, I am ready to make my purchases. Sometimes I decide against everything I thought I wanted. Sometimes I go for broke. Sometimes it is half and half.

This is all about not being pulled too far in any direction. We are all subject to impulses, but if we are aware that we are being carried away, we can redress the balance and return to the fulcrum. From there we can move out when the need arises. We are *level-*

headed—not up in the clouds or down in the doldrums. The point of balance is all-important.

One of the characteristics of the mind is that it is always expecting something, chasing after something it wants, or retreating from or resisting something it doesn't want. It has an extraordinary tendency to slip away from the present moment. And yet it is only in the present that anything happens. All spiritual work takes place in the present at those times when we can disengage from the march of progress or whatever it is that is swiftly carrying us away from where we are. Perhaps the present could be likened to being in neutral, ready to move into another gear but not yet having done so. For a brief period we are "free, free at last." No one can stay in neutral, but it is good to acknowledge that it is from this place that the next move comes and to this place that it will eventually return. This is the common ground. If we succeed in remaining still with a situation, a decision, or a problem, instead of scurrying after various distractions, both the mind and heart will open, and unlooked-for opportunities will emerge.

The other night I was caught unawares. I had two guests to supper, and shortly after they arrived, my phone rang. It was Adam's girlfriend asking if he was with me. She had just returned home from work, it was 7.45 P.M., and there was no message from him. This was an unusual situation. Adam is very responsible, and I don't remember any occasion when such a thing had happened before. If he is going to be late, he always calls ahead. I suggested that he might be stuck in the subway, but she uses the same line and had not had any difficulty getting home herself. She had already tried his office, and he wasn't there. Not knowing what else to suggest, I simply asked that he call me when he did arrive home. As soon as I hung up, I started to panic. Earlier in the day he had called to say that he was not feeling at all well, and I counseled him to phone the doctor immediately. So now I envisioned him lying unconscious somewhere.

I tried to bring myself back to the dining room table and the conversation going on around it. I struggled to be a good hostess, but in vain. I was grateful for the demand on my attention, for the company, and for the support it provided, but I felt myself so far from what was taking place in the room that I could no longer connect to it. I was distraught, undone, frozen.

My mind went wild, scrabbling around like a frightened animal, and paralysis set in.

Why is it that it is so difficult to accept the condition of not knowing? The times when all there is to do is wait are so hard. Energy arises to meet the need— any need—and the system is flooded, overwhelmed. So it simply shuts down.

Over the years there have been many occasions when I have stood silently at the window watching what was going on in the street below. Sometimes, years ago, I was waiting for my ex-husband and our toddler son to return from the beach. As each light changed and their taxi didn't appear, I would try to calm myself and wait for the next light, the next cab to slow down across from our building. Sometimes I would wait there for an hour and they wouldn't arrive, and I would try not to think of what disasters might have overtaken them. Sometimes I stood there waiting in vain for my lover to return. The truth is that I have stood there over and over again in different situations, but always the people I was expecting have eventually arrived and no harm has befallen them. Still, this time it might be different . . . Fear is always lurking around the corner.

On this occasion, Adam turned up after an hour. He had thought that his girlfriend was arriving home from work later. He had gone to a video store and lost track of the time. He seemed taken aback that we had been worrying about him. As soon as I knew that he was safe and that nothing was wrong, I lay down on the sofa and closed my eyes, allowing all the anxiety to seep away. I became aware that one of the women had her arms gently around me and that the other one was clearing the dishes. I just let go.

Somehow I, we, need to learn to let go at the beginning and not just at the end. We have to find a way to remain centered. This is a big lesson that most of us put off learning all our lives.

There is something in the third chapter of Genesis that addresses the question of fear and presence. Remember when God calls to Adam and says, "Where art thou?" and Adam responds, "I heard thy voice in the garden, and I was afraid, because I was naked; and I hid myself." This is the first time in the Bible that God asks man where he is. Until then, presumably, this had not been necessary because Adam and Eve were simply present. But once they had eaten of the fruit of the tree of knowledge of good and evil, they wandered and their minds wandered, and both God and they no longer knew where they were. Once fear enters, we are no longer present. Fear is fear of the unknown. In the present, fear doesn't exist.

There is actually a reference in the next chapter that I have always found both fascinating and relevant. It says, "And Cain went out from the presence of the Lord and dwelt in the land of Nod." When I was studying Hebrew I discovered that the word *nod* means "restless" or "wandering." I don't know why the word was not translated in the King James version. Giving it a capital letter like that makes us think that it is a country in its own right. I believe that what is meant here is that after killing his brother, Cain no longer knew how to be still and in the present moment, and that he became a wanderer, or nomad.

I always have the sense that traveling in a plane is very similar to being out of gear. The moment a plane lifts off the runway into the air is a moment of sheer delight. My heart experiences a release—of attachment to the ground, perhaps—and I am filled with a deep smile. Once you are up above the clouds with their fleeces turned toward the sun, you are in a hiatus, having left one place and not yet reached your destination.

This in itself can be a very liberating experience. On one such journey to London about twenty years ago, I made the following observation:

I have just seen that it is attachment and identification that prevent true work. When one is content and there is no desire, no preoccupation claiming the light and strength of consciousness, then the mind naturally dwells in the present. Desire exists only when tied to a future, not-yet-arrived moment. The subtle attachment to an illusion is what produces tension—a net drawn tightly across the surface of the mind preventing entry.

We have all had the experience of trying to do something while our attention was still on something else, and thoughts seemed to bounce off our minds. It is only later that we realize that we were not open to whatever needed to be done. Recently someone brought me a publicity release to check through. I had been in an all-day meeting and was on the phone to an author. I read through the release and made a few grammatical corrections, but it was not until the following day at home that I came to and remembered that the reason for publishing the book in question had been completely omitted from the release. I had been so caught up in what I had been doing in addition to everything that still had to be done that I had forgotten to come into the present. The lines of tension surrounded me and prevented me from appreciating the situation clearly.

Perhaps the reason so many of us feel driven by exterior circumstances, be it household chores or the volume and intensity of our workload, is that we often have a fixed idea of what we still have to do (or are avoiding thinking about it) and when we believe we should get it all done. None of us can measure up to this "tyranny of the shoulds." For some strange reason, we have the impression that everyone else is living a perfectly ordered life, even though it is obvious that they are not. We all have things that never quite get done, but the truth is that however long you live and however hard you work, you cannot finish everything. Susan Strasser's history of American housework expresses this perfectly. It is called *Never Done*.

Some of the pressure we feel comes from the fact that we focus on what we haven't accomplished rather than what we have. My friend Sarah Jane once pointed out that after God had worked for six days, he saw that everything he had made was very good and he ceased (*shavat*) from his labor, but that is not what we do. Almost all of us don't see or don't admit that what we have done is good (let alone very good), and we rarely stop working because we believe that whatever we have done is not quite good enough. The concept of a Sabbath, first described in the Book of Genesis, was and still is a revolutionary one. It is important to stop at a certain point, no matter what is happening.

Observing the Sabbath is in many ways like practicing meditation. When I began to meditate, it seemed as though I could not possibly fit it into my already busy life, but I found that if I put it first, then a measure of rest entered my life and from that place I was able to move on, refreshed and restored. It was as though the day expanded to accommodate these two half-hours.

It is the same with reserving one day a week for respite, one day when nothing is scheduled and we are free to delight in whatever arises—a day to acknowledge the divine and be glad. On this day we focus not on doing but on being.

It is our addiction to "doing" that causes much of the trouble and all the frenzy. We cram more and more into our days, and none of it ultimately satisfies us because we ourselves are the driving force behind it, seeking to achieve this and that, and coming up empty-handed every time. All this activity doesn't bring us the serenity and contentment we seek. It just exhausts us. If we stop to think about it, whatever it is will either get done or it won't. If we were to die today, either someone else would take care of it or not.

It is the claim that we put on this doing that is the problem. Somewhere deep inside us we believe that we are what we do. We identify with our actions. We invest ourselves in every action, under the illusion that if we are not doing something, then perhaps we don't exist. *Invest* means "clothe in." It is a habit, something we don. Somehow, we persuade ourselves that it is *our* responsibility to do every job. We become identified with both the work and the results. But the truth is that it is not *our* work; it is *the* work. If we can find a way to relax our grip on our actions and what comes out of them, there is great freedom. Just watching the activity rather than becoming completely identified with it is restful rather than exhausting. Nowadays people will claim almost any work they think they have to do. I hear people say that they have to do a wash when what they mean is that they have to carry laundry to the washing machine and press a button. However, because they believe that *they* are doing the washing, they may be using up as much energy as they would if they had to go down to the river and beat the sheets on a rock.

The space in the mind that I refer to from time to time has many blessed qualities. In a way, it is this space that is the fabric of the universe. Everything we do happens in this space.

> *Thirty spokes share the wheel's hub;*
> *It is the center hole that makes it useful.*
> *Shape clay into a vessel;*
> *It is the space within that makes it useful.*
> *Cut doors and windows for a room;*
> *It is the holes which make it useful.*
> *Therefore benefit comes from what is there;*
> *Usefulness from what is not there.*
>
> —*Tao Te Ching*, by Lao Tsu, chapter 11

In the Hindu tradition there are five elements: earth, water, fire, air, and ether, or space. Space is often the element that is overlooked, and yet it is the one we yearn for—the one where we feel at home. Without space, there would be no place for the other elements to manifest themselves. Or, to put it another way, without a "here" there can be no "now." Once we begin to catch sight of our desires and then let go of them, we can take an extra step: We can actually rest. It has been said that true rest takes place only between one desire and the next, between the moment when you have relinquished one thought and before you have been hooked by the next. When worries awake me in the middle of the night, it is obvious that I have not been resting. I was not able to surrender my problems before I went to sleep. I am not resting either in my bed or in the infinity of space.

THIRTEEN

Law and Order

There is a strong tradition of cleaning in my family. Most likely it started with our Victorian nanny, Miss Rizpah Smith (known to one and all as Moth because one of the incipient maharajahs she had looked after in India felt that her white hair made her look like a moth). It continued at boarding school, became honed at work parties at the philosophy school, and is now second nature. I have always suspected it is true that cleanliness is next to godliness.

As you have probably gathered, things in my house are neat and orderly. Moth used to come to stay with us when we had grown up, and she always said that looking into my closets made her uncomfortable because they were so tidy. My rejoinder was that she had only herself to blame because I would never have learned this skill without her.

Some people probably find my passion for having everything in its place a little unreasonable, but I simply cannot rest if my apartment or desk is messy. Once my surroundings are in order, my thoughts are sorted out too. Leaving everything ready for its next use means that you do not have to worry about what you have left undone. If you come to visit me, you will never catch me unprepared. I would not dream of going out in the morning without having made my bed. I do not go to sleep at night without washing the supper dishes. If a garment gets stained or torn, I clean or mend it the same day. Readiness is all. I understand that it may be hard for other people to be this organized, and I certainly don't expect it of them, but I can report that it does wonders for your mind—and perhaps even for your heart.

Neil once told me about a woman he knew who couldn't face ironing. She used to stash all the wrinkled clothes in the closet, and at one point when she hadn't ironed for three months, she had to take a running jump at the door to get it closed. This tale sounded apocryphal to me because I simply couldn't imagine such a situation.

When Adam was a teenager and from time to time I got him to tidy up and clean his room, he would admit (without prompting) that he felt a great deal better afterward and he didn't even know the principle behind what I had asked him to do. I was never able to understand how he managed to do any homework in his room the way it usually looked. As I get older, it's so easy to lose track of things that if I do not put them in the right place to begin with, I may never find them again. And even when I do put them in the right place, they seem to walk off sometimes.

In my experience what goes on inside us is reflected on the outside, and vice versa. Perhaps they are two aspects of the same thing. You can either clean up your act in what we think of as the real world and this will clarify what is within, or you can work from the other direction.

Whenever I see a layer of dust on my dining room table or sideboard, I have to take care of it or I will have the distinct impression that the dust will settle into my mind. Still, I do not see this as a chore. I actually feel that I am burnishing my mind each time I clean. When I go to visit my mother and her home is not as pristine as mine, I am concerned not just for her exterior health but for her inner health too. I want her to have as much clarity as possible in her last years. I don't explain why I am cleaning, but I was really touched on my last visit when my sister-in-law, Valery, came to see us and commented on the lightness she found that hadn't been there before. We all know how grungy we feel when we enter a room that hasn't been cleaned for a long time.

Sometimes the way to clear the cobwebs from your mind is to take a brisk walk outside. It has been snowing on and off for the last few days and my body hasn't felt like volunteering for exercise, but today the sun was bright and the sky blue and I practically danced down the street as I went in search of ink cartridges and dark-chocolate cookies. Now here I am back in front of the screen, and I have the energy to write once more. Even if you can't go outside, when you find yourself falling asleep over what you are doing or reaching an impasse, get up and do some physical movement. I find that cleaning always does the trick. If I get stuck on this page for too long, I shall go to the hall closet and do a little spring-cleaning. As I hung up my jacket just now, I noticed that fluff was accumulating on the floor between the shoes.

In some ways I see my editorial function as one of cleaning and polishing. I am not one of those editors who dream up ideas for books. I take the Michelangelo approach: If you offer me a block of Carrara marble (and it does have to be the best quality), then I can see the David within and help the author carve his or her vision out of the block of stone. I had one author who used to say that I edited his mind rather than his manuscript. Obviously, if you can do your editorial work there, there is less to do with a pencil later.

When I was growing up my mother would often say, "Don't throw away dirty water until you have clean," and I believed her. I don't know where this maxim came from, but recently I started thinking about it and realized that it doesn't make any sense. As long as your basin is full of dirty water, there is nowhere to put clean water, and there is also little chance that anyone will offer you any. While you are holding on to one object, your hands are not free to accept something else. While you have one idea firmly in place, it is impossible to entertain another.

Perhaps it is the inclination to have everything ready and available that enables me to be prompt for appointments. There is nothing dragging me back or holding me down. I am not running behind as so many people seem to be. In fact, I have an annoying habit of arriving early no matter how late I start off. I really do try to be late but I have rarely succeeded, and on the few occasions when circumstances like the traffic conspire against me, I do not worry because I know in my heart that if I am going to be late, other people will be even later.

I used to get upset when someone I was meeting for lunch was late at the restaurant, particularly if the wait lasted more than fifteen minutes. But eventually I realized that this hiatus was a gift. I was already in place, and there was nothing else to do but rest. For once, I didn't have to go anywhere or do anything. When the other person finally turns up, you can be much more gracious about it, whatever his or her excuse, if you see the time alone as a plus rather than a minus.

One of the concepts in Judaism that continues to fascinate me is that of *tikkun olam*. This expression from the Hebrew root *TKN*, "to set straight or put in order," is generally translated as "repair, restoration, or healing of the world," the idea being that we are here on this earth in order to look after whatever has gone awry or needs mending. But I think of it more in terms of our being caretakers. The word *caretaker* is used to describe someone who is responsible either for a sick or elderly person or for a building. In reality, the word has a much richer meaning. A caretaker is someone who takes care, who is careful, i.e., full of care. This puts a different complexion on the concept. It implies that our function is to care for one another and the whole of creation however we can. It means that our attention naturally goes out to other people and things wherever it is needed. There is a quality of devotion about it that doesn't normally come to mind when we say "caretaker."

Lately, I have been rereading the first five books of the Bible, studying both the English and the Hebrew texts, which is very rewarding. Each time, one comes across something new. What I discovered this time was that the Hebrew verb *shamar,* meaning "watch over, care for, protect, give attention to, observe, and revere," is used in (at least) four significant places. The first time is in Genesis 2:15 when God tells Adam to "till and care for" the Garden of Eden. In Genesis 4:9 comes Cain's famous response, "Am I my brother's keeper?" It turns out that "keeper," as it is usually translated, is not very accurate. The word really means "caretaker" or "someone who watches out for you." Then, in Genesis 28:15, in the passage about Jacob's dream, God says, "Remember, I am with you: I will protect you wherever you go . . ." And I had not realized that in the second rendering of the Ten Commandments, in Deuteronomy 5:12, the instruction regarding the Sabbath day is to "observe" it rather than "remember" it, as it says in Exodus. So it turns out that caring is what we are here in this world to do for one another. God cares for, protects, and watches over us, and, in the same way, we do this for others in whatever way we can.

On my bedroom wall is a calligraphed and illuminated quote by the Tibetan Buddhist teacher Chögyam Trungpa, which says:

> Generosity is giving whatever you have. It is not for you to make judgments; it is for the recipients to make the gesture of receiving. If the recipients are not ready for your generosity, they will not receive it.

This ties in closely with the Jewish practice of *tzedakah*, which is often translated as "charity," but, in fact, the two concepts are different. *Charity*, as described in the New Testament, is choosing to give to someone when you perceive his or her need. It has an optional quality about it. *Tzedakah*, on the other hand, comes from the root meaning "wise" or "just." In Judaism, *tzedakah* is a requirement. (I believe that taking care of the poor is also one of the Five Pillars of Islam.) What this means is that if you are on the subway and a scruffy man asks you for a handout, you don't size him up and decide whether or not he deserves it. You simply give. There is no way you can know for certain what his situation is, and the rabbis taught that it is better to err on the side of generosity. God forbid you should refuse the one person in dire need.

This is not easy to put into practice. When I first learned about *tzedakah*, I was very moved and for the next week or so, I was able to just give, whoever asked me. But gradually this goodwill dissipated, and I started to judge people again. It was particularly hard when I went to India where women clutching babies drag on your arm, beseeching you for money, and when you relent and give them some, they ask for more. They figure that if you have already given something, you undoubtedly have more available and the next person may not. Also, in their culture, there is more merit in giving than receiving, so the way they see it, they are doing you a favor by allowing you to give again. This is hard for Westerners to grasp, particularly since no thanks are ever forthcoming. I didn't mind giving, but I wasn't able to resist feeling entitled to some kind of acknowledgment!

Of course, this is related to the idea that none of us really owns anything. Everything currently in my possession is just passing through my hands. I have been entrusted with it, or, to put it another way, I am its caretaker. Through the luck of the draw I was born into more favorable circumstances than millions of other people. I have never gone hungry or been without a roof over my head. Trungpa said, "Generosity is giving whatever you have." No equivocation there.

Here is one of my favorite stories about the Buddha. He was teaching one day, when someone started to heckle him. The Buddha stopped and asked the man: "If someone offers you a wonderful gift and you refuse it, to whom does the gift belong?" The man answered that it would remain the property of the giver. "Even so," said the Buddha, "I do not accept your abuse." It is said that the man's attitude was so changed that he became one of the Buddha's disciples.

This morning I admitted to myself that I was unlikely to ever again wear the pinafore dress I wore last Thursday. For some reason, although I was delighted with it when I bought it, it no longer suits me, and I know that it will lurk in my closet forevermore unless I Take Steps. So I extracted it and looked along the rack to see what else might join it on a trip to what my tax accountant calls "the Slavation Army" (What does he know that I don't?). I managed to put together a good shopping bag–ful of clothes that others might like. It is amazing how often you can do this and still find garments you are no longer attached to. But the miraculous effect of this surrendering and clearing out is the space that it creates. It is the space in and around things that is so wondrous. We all know that when our closets and drawers are crammed full, we cannot tell what is in them. When there is sufficient space to see what is there, we have a real choice about what to wear because we are able to get a clear view.

It is also healthy to relinquish larger items. Once I had both a child and a job, I started using the piano as a receptacle for manuscripts rather than for making music, and it sat there month after month like a reproach. One day a colleague came to dinner and admired it. I asked her if she played, and she said that she would if she had a piano. So I offered it to her. I explained that having something that large in the corner of the living room not being put to the use for which it was intended was a minus for me rather than a plus. She would be doing me a big favor by taking it away and putting it to good use. I also gave her the piano stool and my music.

What I sense is happening during this period of my life is a gradual draining or spring-cleaning of my mind, as I let go of one thing after another, whether it is attachment to particular garments or long-held ideas about people or things. In their stead, I find that from time to time an idea or a small revelation will drift in. It arrives on its own and doesn't come confused with a multitude of other stuff, so I am able to appreciate it fully and decide how to make the best use of it.

The important lesson here is to see what you can leave out of your life. If you consider music, for example, it is obvious that the space between the notes makes all the difference——both how wide the interval is and how long the silence lasts. It isn't any different with your clothes and, indeed, all your possessions. There is an inordinate amount of freedom to be found in giving things up.

FOURTEEN

Traveling Light

Once we are born, only two things are certain. One is that we will die and the other that we will experience change. In *The Mahabharata*, Prince Arjuna is asked, "What is the greatest wonder in the world?" and his response is, "Each day death strikes, and yet we live as if we were immortal." Nothing in the universe stands still, so why is it that we are so often surprised by change and shocked by death? The whole of this book is about ways in which we can live more freely in the universe, without most of the stuff we generally carry around. This is, in some measure, a preparation for our final journey. But this particular chapter is about preparing for all the other journeys we take in this life.

Many of the changes in our lives appear to be thrust upon us, but there are also those times when we deliberately seek out change. The most obvious occasion is when we travel. Nowadays many of us find ourselves on the road or in the air at frequent intervals. Travel has become a "fixture" in our lives, and we do not always acknowledge its implications.

Whether we are going away on business, for pleasure, out of obligation, or as recreation, leaving the comfort of our own home causes an upheaval, even if it offers some measure of respite. For a time you are separated and released from customary chores and routines, but being in an unfamiliar environment entails other forms of stress.

The way I deal with this is to create a small comfort cocoon, in much the same way that astronauts do as they rove the skies. If you take a survival kit along with you, it provides an insurance you can always fall back on. The makeup of this kit will differ from person to person, from one location to another, and also according to the season. In the 1960s many girls would not leave home without their eyelash curlers. The main thing is to take with you whatever will enable you to settle into and enjoy your new surroundings without fretting over something you feel is indispensable but lacking. I once lived with a man unencumbered enough to carry whatever he needed in a waist pack, but most of us are under the impression that we cannot manage with just a comb, a toothbrush, and our ID.

If we are traveling because of our work or in response to a family crisis, we are relatively clear as to the purpose of our trip, but this isn't always the case when we are "just getting away from it all."

What are we looking for when we go on vacation? Isn't it a break from our life in general? We want a change of scene, different circumstances, another view of the world, perhaps a new passion of some kind.

I find it interesting that Americans go on vacation while the British go on holiday. The original meaning of each of these words is quite different. *Vacation* comes from the Latin and has to do with emptiness and freedom, while the Old English *holiday* is a day or time dedicated to the sacred, wholeness, and health. Maybe the reason I prefer to go on holiday rather than on vacation is that I am English, but I suspect it is because the promise of what I might receive on holiday is far greater than what I might get on vacation.

It is important to be clear about the aim of your journey. Some people like to go back to the same place every year. I assume what they are looking for is comforting and familiar surroundings where they can relax and regroup. Others, like me, have something very different in mind. We want to stretch all our muscles—physical, mental, emotional, and spiritual. This often means that the beds and the food are not as wonderful as we would like but it offers so many other possibilities that it is always worth the trade-off, and sometimes the accommodations do turn out to be good. Many people dream of going to a particular place, but they don't think it through any further than that. This is rather like planning your wedding but not having any idea of what marriage itself is. It makes sense, therefore, to prepare for the trip, however long it may be, so that you can take full advantage of your time away once you are there.

I am drawn to places where I think I will be nourished on every level. I don't go to great lengths to seek out these places. I use the same method as I do as an editor. With books, I keep an open and welcoming mind, and they arrive out of the blue. My vacation decisions come about in much the same way. Two weeks ago I opened a magazine and saw an advertisement for a trip to Turkey "On the Path of Rumi" and knew immediately that I would go on it. For many years I had wanted to go to Turkey, but it had somehow never worked out. When opportunities like this present themselves, don't hesitate.

Over the years I have visited the Golden Ring churches and monasteries in the countryside around Moscow, spent the turn of the millennium at St. Peter's in Rome with the pope (and ten thousand other pilgrims), explored arts and crafts on the enchanted island of Bali, traced the River Ganges to its source in the Himalayas, traveled with a group of Buddhists to practice centers in the southwestern United States, gone on a nine-day silent retreat in California, and made a short trip to a small town in Germany to be in the presence of Mother Meera, a young Indian woman considered by many to be an incarnation of the Divine Mother. In each case I was seeking to reconnect my spirit with the ground of my being, so that I could return home refreshed and invigorated, and in some measure this always happened.

When we are in new surroundings it is easier for us to see and hear more clearly. We don't labor under the impression that we have "seen it all before." When I got to Bali, I wished I had not boned up ahead of time by reading the Insight Guide. The full-color photos in the guide were so good that when I saw the actual places, I was rather disappointed because I felt I already knew what they looked like. It is always a toss-up about how much to read before you go. On my recent trip to China, I was so overwhelmed at the size of the country and the fact that I had no knowledge of the language and very little of its history that I threw up my hands and did nothing. I landed in Beijing in a state of tabula rasa, and everything I drank in was wondrously new. Generally, I riffle through a guidebook and read one or two other books to give me some background before I set off. This provides a context for whatever happens once I arrive.

I always hope for the kind of experience that happened to me in an industrial town called Ningbo on the eastern coast of China. An old Chinese friend in

Connecticut had asked me to see if I could buy him a Chinese edition of the classic Zen collection of koans, *The Blue Cliff Record*. I marched into a three-story bookstore near my hotel and tried to find someone who spoke English. People looked at me in complete incomprehension but kept pointing upward (where it turned out the foreign-language books were) so I moved from escalator to escalator, always hoping that there would be someone with whom I could communicate. After fifteen minutes of nonsuccess, I came across two girls about age fourteen, one of whom said, "I speak English," and they tried to help me. As I discovered much later, the name of the book in Chinese is nothing like *The Blue Cliff Record*, and so no one recognized the ideographs Kaz had written on my little piece of paper. But just before I left the store, one of the girls asked me, "What are you doing here? Why are you here?" I was rather taken aback and didn't know how to answer. She was asking what I was doing in Ningbo of all places, but her question aroused a deeper question within me: What was I doing here (or anywhere, for that matter) and why? I find that being away from home often puts me in wake-up situations like this, and I am grateful.

Whether I am going away for twenty-four hours, a weekend, or much longer, once I have left home, I am on my way. This may sound obvious, but what I mean is that once I have locked the door to my apartment, everything that has gone before is in the past. I don't carry my ordinary life with me in my head. I do indeed vacate (in some respects I have become an American). I can travel an hour's distance to stay with a friend and not think twice all the time I am away of the things that normally occupy me, so that sometimes twenty-four hours is all the break I need. When I go to a foreign country, it is sometimes hard for me to remember my job and my family back home. People will ask what books I am working on, and I cannot dredge up a single title.

I always carry with me a mini-notebook that fits into the palm of my hand, and when I am on vacation I make brief notes as I travel. I have bad camera karma, and so I have not bothered with photos for many years. My father once lent me his Nikon and I dutifully took thirty-six shots of Norway, only to find when I had them developed that the roller had stuck on the first frame. I felt as though I had missed Norway while looking through the lens, and I determined that I would never waste my holiday in this way again.

So nowadays I just scribble down a phrase here and there to remind me of a scene or something fascinating that I hear. This kind of shorthand enables me to write up a twenty-page journal of the trip on my return. Nowadays I have a small army of people who travel with me vicariously. They say that they are glad that I am making these trips and not them. They can enjoy traveling without leaving their armchairs. My Chinese professor friend and his wife have even put in a request for me to go to the Galápagos Islands because they feel that they are now too old to journey there themselves but they would still like to go (I declined. That part of the world doesn't speak to me—yet).

I have tried to keep this book free of instructions on how to do this or that on the physical level, because there are already many books available that provide that kind of advice. However, friends and traveling companions always marvel at how lightly I travel. So, by popular demand, I am including my checklist of travel essentials that I keep handy for those stressful days just before you set off on a journey. If you have a list like this, you don't have to wonder what you might be forgetting. Of course, your list will look slightly different from mine (particularly if you are a man), so just use this one as a model and make up a list of your own.

As you will see, I plan for every eventuality. You never know these days how unpredictable the weather will be or what pickle you will find yourself in, such as an extra eight hours on the runway, so it is best to be prepared.

Don't travel with more than you can lift (or trundle). There might not be anyone to help you at the other end. Also, it is far safer to take the suitcase into the plane with you than entrust it to airline personnel. Airlines lose track of your luggage at the most inconvenient times. Well, I suppose that there really are no convenient times for losing luggage.

Some years ago I flew to India on Gulf Air, and we changed planes in Bahrain. It had been an interminable journey, and we arrived in Delhi at 5 A.M. on a Sunday morning only to discover that all our luggage (there were twenty-five in the party) had remained in Bahrain and wouldn't arrive for another forty-eight hours. One official with a blunt pencil was detailed to fill in the forms describing each piece of luggage. This took two hours. While we were awaiting our turn, the tour guide brought us cups of hot chai (the aromatic Indian tea) in thick, chipped cups. I had been warned never to drink anything out of a cup that was not my own unless I was in a hotel or restaurant, because there was no way to tell whether the cup had been washed properly. My own metal cup was, of course, in Bahrain. For about half an hour I hesitated, but when I saw all my fellow travelers drinking and realized that it would be two days before I would meet up with my cup again, I nervously accepted the hot tea. By the time we arrived at the hotel, I had begun to feel very ill. I spent the next two days lying on my bed, shaking from head to foot. I couldn't eat anything and sipped just a little water provided by the hotel when it was absolutely necessary. I hadn't caught any dire disease. It was simply fear. But it prevented me from running around town like the others who were enjoying themselves hugely, buying clothes and other things that they needed to tide them over. The moral of this story is that you should not lose sight of your own luggage. This means packing very economically.

Always keep your toilet bag in a state of readiness, so that you don't have to check it out and make last-minute purchases for necessities you thought you already had. The time to check everything is before you put the bag away at the end of your vacation. Make certain that each little bottle or tube is full enough to last two weeks or however long you usually go away for.

Leave in your suitcase the things that you use only when you travel so that you don't have to collect them from wherever each time. For instance: shoe bags, extra hangers, tea bags, airplane socks, and toilet bag.

And, last, leave room in your suitcase to bring back goodies from your trip. If you have to sit on the suitcase to get it closed before you depart, you are going to be in trouble when you find something irresistible in a market somewhere.

Here is my list:

TRAVELING ESSENTIALS
(This includes what you are wearing)

Alien registration card (I've never become an
American), passport, money, and ticket (including
xeroxes of ARC and passport to be kept in a
separate place. If your passport is lost or stolen,

the agony will be less if you at least have all the
details with you)

Map + list of addresses and telephone numbers of
people to visit in duplicate (keep each list in a
different place so that when you mislay one, you
can still find the other)

Food and water for the journey (Why would you
want to wait until the airline decides to serve its
unnourishing meals?)

Ziploc bags

Dried fruit and nuts (in case the hotel food leaves
something to be desired or an excursion lasts four
hours longer than anticipated)

Tea bags (English breakfast)

Ground coffee and gold filter (it's unlikely that the
coffee will be as good as your own)

Hard candy (for when there's no water)

Strap in case suitcase breaks (mine never has, but it
just might)

Toiletries (including detergent and tissues. Take half
a roll of toilet paper in a plastic bag and keep it in

your purse or pocket. You don't want to be
without in an emergency)

Small and large shoulder bags + money belt (keep
your traveler's checks and spare cash in your money
belt. It's worth the trouble, and you will no longer
feel the belt around your waist after a few hours)

Swimsuit(s) (you never know which hotels will have
good pools or when you might come across a
mountain spring)

Umbrella and raincoat

Laundry bag

3 hangers

2 books

Notebook plus extra pen and pencil

Sunglasses and reading glasses

Sun hat

Alarm clock (check the batteries before you leave)

Flashlight small enough to carry in your purse (ditto)

Washcloth (these are unknown in many foreign climes)

Pull-on slippers for the plane

Warm jacket or coat, gloves, and Polartec headband (in winter)

2 pairs of shoes

2 pairs of socks

Nightgown

Pashmina (no nice Jewish Buddhist would travel without her pashmina shawl)

Jewelry

4 sets of separates that can be mixed and matched (don't include anything that needs ironing)

1 outfit for out-of-season weather (the world climate has already gone berserk, so be prepared)

1 warm overblouse

1 sweater or vest

4 pairs of panty hose

3 undershirts

2 slips (if taking skirts)

5 pairs of underpants

When you pack, you will find you can get more in if you fold things as little as possible. Align both legs of your pants and fold them over just once. Fold sweaters and blouses horizontally, and then fold the sleeves on top. This small step can make a huge difference, not only in the amount of space you save but also in the number of wrinkles the clothes don't have.

The first time I met my editor, Mitch Horowitz, he was very intrigued to see that I was going off to stay with a friend with nothing but a large shoulder bag. He wanted to know how that was possible and asked exactly what was in my purse. This is what I told him:

If I am going for just one night (as I was on that occasion), I figure I can wear the same thing the day I arrive as the day I leave, although normally I wouldn't do this. So all I need are clean underclothes and panty hose or socks, plus a sweater or shawl of some kind because it is usually ten degrees colder in the country than in New York City. My cosmetic case always contains a traveling toothbrush, a tiny tube of toothpaste, lipstick, rouge, face cream, mirror, comb, safety pins, toothpick, aspirin, fold-up scissors, cough lozenges, Band-Aids, a few sheets of toilet paper (and the cosmetic case is small, believe me), so I don't need anything more for one night. I like to sleep in my nothings, so no nightgown is necessary (unless I am staying in a hotel and think I might need to flee from a fire in the night). What else? One book. A pad and paper to write on. An umbrella: I normally carry a fold-up umbrella everywhere with me, so that wouldn't really be extra for the weekend, and I also carry a Japanese fan for unair-conditioned subway cars plus a small flashlight for descending emergency staircases in tall buildings in the dark (I had to do this from the twenty-second floor at my office once and don't want to be caught that way again). I make sure to wear shoes that will work for almost every occasion and are good for walking or loafing in. Oh, and a small gift for my host.

That's it. I don't know why people make such a fuss about packing. I don't like to haul a great deal around with me, and I rarely miss all the things that others seem to bring along, particularly since I have noticed that most people do not actually use much of what they take away with them.

FIFTEEN

In Conclusion

Here is a passage by Abraham Joshua Heschel from *A Passion for Truth*:

All worlds are in need of exaltation, and everyone is charged to lift what is low, to unite what lies apart, to advance what is left behind. . . . All facts are parables; their object is God. All things are tales the Teacher relates in order to render intelligible issues too difficult to comprehend literally, directly. Through things seen, God accommodates Himself to our level of understanding. What a shame it is that people do not comprehend the greatness of things on earth. They act as if life were trivial, not realizing that every trifle is filled with Divinity. No one makes a move that does not stir the highest Heaven.

When a young woman who was my assistant for a brief period came to tell me that she was leaving to go to work for a new magazine, she explained, "You need someone good at detail, which I'm not."

I explained to her gently that there are only details. There isn't anything else. If you step onto a bridge and don't look where you are going, you may lose your footing and plunge into the water. I had earlier tried to get her to understand that it is better to pay attention and get something right to begin with than to make a small mistake and expend a great deal of time and energy correcting it. Mistakes proliferate at an alarming rate. In that last conversation I encouraged her to understand the nature of details not for my sake but for her own. Not paying attention to a detail might one day cost her her life.

It made me a little sad that during the five months she worked for me, she had not learned one of the most important things I had to teach her—scrupulous attention to everything. I have this down to such a fine art that it sometimes backfires! Publishing books is all about detail, and those who work with me sometimes assume that I have checked everything carefully, and therefore (I suspect) they don't double-check what I hand over to them the way they do for other people. They just assume that I have probably caught any mistakes. I am as fallible as everyone else, which is why I feel the need to be so careful. I am never sure that I have caught everything.

Because even the smallest detail is vital, I find it important to keep in mind the four laws of ecology that Barry Commoner shared with the world in his book *The Closing Circle*. They are as useful to me now as they were when I first encountered them in 1971:

1. Everything is connected to everything else.
2. Everything must go somewhere.
3. Nature knows best.
4. There's no such thing as a free lunch.

One of the remarkable aspects of these principles is that they are all saying the same thing, and so it doesn't really matter at which end you start.

Everything that you think or do or say is connected not only to everything else in your life but also to everything in everybody else's life. You cannot do something in isolation, something that does not have an effect on the world at large.

Not only is everything connected to everything else, but each person is also connected to everyone else. We are all joined at the hip, so to speak. Looked at in this way, it becomes evident that there is only one of us. Buddhists explain this by saying that each of us is like a different part of the same body and we tend to strut about, believing that we have a life of our own, although, in truth, we may be just a cell or an eyelash.

The corollary to all this is that not only does what you or I do affect the whole world, but what everyone else in the world does affects us also. This is why it is impossible (at least for us) to trace karma back to its roots. There are strands of it coming from every conceivable direction.

It follows that if someone takes you out for a meal, sends you an armful of tulips, or pays you a compliment, it comes with a price. The price is not necessarily visible on a tag, but it is definitely there. The donor may believe that he or she is giving you something freely, but that may not be the way you receive the gift—or vice versa. There are subtle strings joining everything in creation. I don't mean that you will necessarily "pay back" the same person. The response you have to what you received may take any number of forms. For instance, "random acts of kindness" are not nearly as random as people believe. I heard a story about someone paying the toll for the car behind without knowing who was driving that car. The person who paid the toll did so because of something that had happened to her. And the driver who was on the receiving end undoubtedly passed on the goodwill to someone else in one form or another. As I said, it doesn't have to be a direct quid pro quo.

This is all part of the law of karma. Many people believe that karma is linear: If you do some terrible (or wonderful) thing, you will receive your just desserts. However, the way it seems to be set up is not as personal as that. You have a thought or take some action, and there is a result. The consequences will be experienced, but not necessarily by you, and nobody knows when.

Around the same time that I discovered Barry

Commoner, I started delving into the work of Alan Watts. The first book I read was *The Book on the Taboo Against Knowing Who You Are*, and there is one story he tells in it that is relevant here. He describes a high fence with just a chink in it through which you can peer in order to see what is going on on the other side. If you put your eye close to the chink, you sometimes get a glimpse of whiskers, then a nose, two ears, a body with two legs, two more legs, and finally a tail. Some time later you may see this sequence in reverse order, and you may very well deduce from your observations that whiskers are always followed by a tail. However, if you looked over the fence, you would see at once that it was all part of the same cat.

It becomes apparent that what may look like a thought, a word, or an action, and its eventual consequences is, in reality, all part of the same cat.

This started out as a book on how to live a simple life. What I discovered as I examined the nature of simplicity is that it all depends on integrity and impeccability. If you focus on these two qualities, your life simplifies itself.

The scraps of wisdom I offer here—my glean-ings—have been gathered over many years. Each grain lingered dormant in a crevice of my mind until now. Perhaps you will connect with one of these seeds and store it away for another decade before you, too, actu-ally water it with your attention and it starts to sprout.

The book is a sharing of all that I have received of value. I have tried to record faithfully whatever I thought would be useful to others. I didn't want to have anything left over! I cannot claim that any of it is original, but I hope that some of it may be new to you. As I was nearing the end and scouring my mind for any overlooked seeds, a friend in London sent me the fol-lowing poem that was written by an American over a hundred years ago. He must have been a very frugal fel-low because he set down on one sheet of paper what it has taken me a whole book to say.

To live content with small means,
to seek elegance rather than luxury
and refinement rather than fashion,
to be worthy, not respectable,
and wealthy, not rich,
to study hard, think quietly,

talk gently, act frankly,

to listen to stars and birds,

babes and sages, with open heart,

to hear all cheerfully,

do all bravely,

await occasions,

hurry never—

in a word, to let the spiritual,

unbidden and unconscious,

grow up through the common.

This is to be my symphony.

William Henry Channing (1810–1884)

About the Author

Toinette Lippe was born in London, where she began her publishing career at André Deutsch. In 1964 she came to New York City "for a year," worked at Simon and Schuster for three years, and then at Alfred A. Knopf as reprint rights director and editor. In 1989 she founded Bell Tower, where she has published fifty-five books. *Nothing Left Over* is the first book she has written.